Aural Book 1

Specimen Aural Tests

for Trinity College London exams from 2017

Initial–Grade 5

Published by
Trinity College London Press
trinitycollege.com

Registered in England
Company no. 09726123

Second impression, June 2017

Printed in England by Caligraving Ltd.

Contents

Acknowledgements

Trinity College London Press gratefully acknowledges the contribution of David Gaukroger, Chris Lawry and Paul McClure, who composed the musical examples in this book. We thank Peter Wild for performing the piano on the CD recordings, and also Luise Horrocks, for being our examiner voiceover on the CDs.

Grateful thanks are due to Tim Grant-Jones, author of the previous Aural Book 1, on which this publication is closely modelled.

In addition, thanks are extended to all the teachers, students and examiners around the world whose comments have contributed to the development of this suite of tests.

Introduction

Aural skill - the ability to listen intelligently to music and to understand what has been heard - forms a vital part of the training of musicians at all levels. The assessment of this skill in practical exams ensures that it is developed alongside instrumental or vocal ability.

This book supports the suite of aural tests developed for use in Trinity College London grade exams from 2017. This set is a development of the successful format of the previous set of tests, retaining the practice of using a single piece of music for all questions. By answering a series of questions all based on the same piece of music, candidates will find that they develop their ability to listen with perception; this process is enhanced by sections of the tests which encourage reading skills and eye-to-ear co-ordination.

The format of the tests at Initial to Grade 5 is very similar to that of the previous set, although various revisions have been made to the specifications resulting in a clearer incremental progression of each topic through the grades. For instance, the first test now always focuses on pulse recognition, with a widening range of time signatures as the grades progress.

Using this book:

This book is designed to be used effectively either by teachers during lessons or by candidates themselves at home. As teachers will generally wish to supply their own explanations of the questions, the text is addressed primarily to the candidate.

For each grade the following information is given:

About the test piece – gives the parameters of the test piece, so that candidates understand the features of the piece, and so that teachers may devise further sample tests if they wish.

What the examiner will do – explains how the examiner will run the test, so that candidates can feel at ease in the exam and so that teachers can run the tests in the same way.

What you will be asked to do – explains what the candidate will be asked to do for each question, so that candidates and teachers clearly understand what the task involves.

What the question is for – explains the musical reasons for the question, enabling candidates and teachers to understand the skills being developed and assessed.

Hints – useful tips on how to prepare for and succeed at each test, covering both valuable musical knowledge and practical hints for the exam itself.

Information for teachers – an overview of the rationale for each section of the tests, highlighting the progression of each skill through the grades and giving tips for adapting the tests to ask a wider selection of questions.

At the end of each grade candidates are invited to try the sample tests, either by using the CD or with their teacher playing the questions.

The **Answer Booklet** contains the text and printed music from the CDs so that teachers can play the examples to their pupils. Although written for the piano, many of the questions in the book are playable on single-line instruments, thus allowing effective preparation in all kinds of teaching situations.

Each example is also annotated with answers clearly indicated, so that candidates can be assisted in their preparation by parents or friends with limited (or no) musical knowledge.

The examples use a variety of styles and are suitable for a range of pianistic abilities. They are not exhaustive, but give ample practice material, while the parameters of the test piece are given at each grade to enable teachers to select suitable supplementary material if necessary.

Using the CDs:

Each track contains a complete set of questions including spoken text and music. The text and music for the CDs may be found in the **Answer Booklet**, along with answers to the questions.

Initial

About the test piece:

metre	$\frac{2}{4}$
length	four bars
key	major
note values	minim, crotchet, quaver
style	single line melody in treble clef
dynamics	all *forte* or all *piano*
articulation	all *staccato* or all *legato*

All questions will be based on the same piece of music.

Question 1

What the examiner will do:

Play the melody three times.

What you will be asked to do:

Clap the pulse on the third playing, stressing the strong beat.

What the question is for:

- To learn to recognise and respond to a **regular pulse**.
- To recognise **where each bar begins.**

Hints

- Each bar has two beats. Listen for the first beat of each bar, which is stronger than the second beat.
- Remember that one note might last for two beats, and that two notes might fit into one beat. Get used to the different rhythms which can fill a bar of $\frac{2}{4}$ time using the note values listed for this level. Make sure that you maintain a firm and regular pulse whatever the rhythm.
- Remember to make the first beat of each bar really clear by clapping or tapping it much more loudly than the other beat. Try using a big hand movement for the strong beat, and a smaller hand movement for the weak beat.
- You don't have to wait until the third playing to try out your clapping. You will be marked on the third playing only, so you can try out your answer during the first and second playings.

Question 2

What the examiner will do:

Play the melody once.

What you will be asked to do:

Tell the examiner whether the melody was played *forte* or *piano*.

What the question is for:

- To develop your skills in recognising **volume (dynamics)**.
- To learn the **words** to describe what you hear.

Hints

- The melody will either be played loudly throughout or softly throughout.
- The Italian word for loud is **forte**, and the Italian word for soft is **piano.**

Question 3

What the examiner will do:

Play the melody once.

What you will be asked to do:

Tell the examiner whether the melody was played *legato* or *staccato*.

What the question is for:

- To develop your skills in recognising **how the music is being played.**
- To learn the **words** to describe what you hear.

Hints

- **Legato** means that the notes are played **smoothly**, with no gaps between them.
- **Staccato** means that the notes are played **detached** – they will sound short and crisp, with space between them.

Question 4

What the examiner will do:

Play the first three notes of the melody once.

What you will be asked to do:

Tell the examiner which of the three notes was the highest, or which was the lowest.

What the question is for:

- To develop your skills in recognising **higher and lower pitch.**
- To improve your ability to **remember pitch.**

Hints

- **Sing the notes** in your head or, if you prefer, sing or hum the notes out loud. Don't worry – the examiner won't be listening to your singing voice; they are only interested in your answer.

Try the tests

CD1 01 - 14

Listen to the CD or ask your teacher to play the tests for you. Each track on the CD contains a complete set of questions. The answers to the tests can be found on pages 3-4 of the **Answer Booklet.**

Grade 1

About the test piece:

metre	$\frac{2}{4}$ or $\frac{3}{4}$
length	four bars
key	major
note values	dotted minim, minim, dotted crotchet, crotchet and quaver
style	single line melody in treble clef
dynamics	all *forte* or all *piano*
articulation	all *staccato* or all *legato*

All questions will be based on the same piece of music.

Question 1

What the examiner will do:

Play the melody three times.

What you will be asked to do:

Clap the pulse on the third playing, stressing the strong beat.

What the question is for:

- To learn to recognise and respond to a **regular pulse.**
- To recognise whether beats are grouped in **twos or threes.**
- To recognise **where each bar begins.**

Hints

- Listen for the first beat of each bar. If each down beat (the strong first beat of the bar) is followed by **one** weak beat, then the time signature is $\frac{2}{4}$. If each down beat is followed by **two** weak beats, then the time signature is $\frac{3}{4}$.
- Remember that notes might last for more than one beat, and that more than one note might fit into one beat. Get used to the various different rhythms which can fill a bar of each time signature using the note values listed for Grade 1. Make sure that you maintain a firm and regular pulse whatever the rhythm.
- Remember to make the first beat of each bar really clear by clapping or tapping it much more loudly than the other beat or beats. Try using a big hand movement for the strong beat, and a smaller hand movement for the weaker beat or beats.
- Remember that the examiner will not ask you the time signature, but will hear your answer from the pattern of your clapping.
- You don't have to wait until the third playing to try out your clapping. You will be marked on the third playing only, so you can try out your answer during the first and second playings.

Question 2

What the examiner will do:

Play the melody once.

What you will be asked to do:

i) Tell the examiner whether the melody was played *forte* or *piano*.
ii) Tell the examiner whether the melody was played *legato* or *staccato*.

What the question is for:

- To develop your skills in recognising **how the music is being played.**
- To learn the **words** to describe what you hear.

Hints

- The melody will either be played loudly throughout or softly throughout.
- The Italian word for loud is **forte**, and the Italian word for soft is **piano**.
- **Legato** means that the notes are played **smoothly**, with no gaps between them. **Staccato** means that the notes are played **detached** – they will sound short and crisp, with space between them.

Question 3

What the examiner will do:

Play the first two bars of the melody once.

What you will be asked to do:

Tell the examiner whether the last note is higher or lower than the first note.

What the question is for:

- To develop your skills in recognising **higher and lower pitch.**
- To improve your ability to **remember pitch.**

Hints

- There is a similar question for Initial, but at Grade 1 you will need to listen to the first two bars rather than just the first three notes.
- **Sing the notes** in your head or, if it helps, sing or hum the notes out loud as they are played. Sing the first and last notes more deliberately to help you hear them clearly.
- Afterwards, sing the last note, then the first one. This will help you know in which direction the notes moved. Don't worry – the examiner won't be listening to your singing voice; they are only interested in your answer.

Question 4

What the examiner will do:

Play the melody twice, first as originally heard then with one change to the rhythm or to the pitch.

What you will be asked to do:

Raise a hand to show the examiner where the change occurs.

What the question is for:

- To develop your **musical memory**.
- To develop your **awareness of rhythm and pitch**.

Hints

- If it helps, **sing or hum** along with the piano when the melody is played the first time. When the melody is played the second time it is better just to listen for the change.
- As soon as you hear the change, let the examiner know by **raising your hand clearly and confidently**.
- Remember that you don't have to describe the change, only to show where it is.

Try the tests

CD1 15 - 28

Listen to the CD or ask your teacher to play the tests for you. Each track on the CD contains a complete set of questions. The answers to the tests can be found on pages 5-8 of the **Answer Booklet**.

Grade 2

About the test piece:

metre	$\frac{2}{4}$ or $\frac{3}{4}$
length	four bars
key	major or minor
note values	dotted minim, minim, dotted crotchet, crotchet, dotted quaver, quaver and semiquaver
style	single line melody in treble clef
dynamics	played with specific dynamic changes (either *forte-piano* or *piano-forte*)
articulation	all *staccato* or all *legato*

All questions will be based on the same piece of music.

Question 1

What the examiner will do:

Play the melody three times.

What you will be asked to do:

Clap the pulse on the third playing, stressing the strong beat.

What the question is for:

- To learn to recognise and respond to a **regular pulse.**
- To recognise whether beats are grouped in **twos or threes.**
- To recognise **where each bar begins.**

Hints

- Listen for the first beat of each bar. If each down beat (the strong first beat of the bar) is followed by **one** weak beat, then the time signature is $\frac{2}{4}$. If each down beat is followed by **two** weak beats, then the time signature is $\frac{3}{4}$.
- Remember that notes might last for more than one beat, and more than one note might fit into one beat. Get used to the various different rhythms which can fill a bar of each time signature using the note values listed for Grade 2. Make sure that you maintain a firm and regular pulse whatever the rhythm.
- Remember to make the first beat of each bar really clear by clapping or tapping it much more loudly than the other beat or beats. Try using a big hand movement for the strong beat, and a smaller hand movement for the weak beat.
- Remember that the examiner will not ask you the time signature, but will hear your answer from the pattern of your clapping.
- You don't have to wait until the third playing to try out your clapping. You will be marked on the third playing only, so you can try out your answer during the first and second playings.

Question 2

What the examiner will do:

Play the melody once.

What you will be asked to do:

i) Tell the examiner the dynamic level at the start and how it changed during the melody.
ii) Tell the examiner whether the melody was played *legato* or *staccato*.

What the question is for:

- To develop your skills in recognising **how the music is being played.**
- To learn the **words** to describe what you hear.

Hints

- The melody will either start loudly and change to a soft volume halfway through, or will begin softly and change to a loud volume halfway through.
- Remember that the Italian word for loud is **forte**, and the word for soft is **piano**.
- **Legato** means that the notes are played smoothly, with no gaps between them. **Staccato** means that the notes are played detached – they will sound short and crisp, with space between them.

Question 3

What the examiner will do:

Play the melody once.

What you will be asked to do:

Tell the examiner whether the last note was higher or lower than the first note.

What the question is for:

- To develop your skills in recognising **higher and lower pitch.**
- To improve your ability to **remember pitch.**

Hints

- There is a similar question for Grade 1, but at Grade 2 you will need to listen to the whole melody rather than just the first two bars. If you require extra practice try the Grade 1 examples again.
- If it helps, **sing or hum the notes** as they are played. Sing the first and last notes more deliberately to help you hear them clearly.
- Afterwards, sing the last note, then the first one, as if starting the melody again. Don't worry – the examiner won't be listening to your singing voice; they are only interested in your answer.

Question 4

What the examiner will do:

Play the melody twice, first as originally heard and then with one change to the rhythm or to the pitch.

What you will be asked to do:

i) Raise a hand to show the examiner where the change occurs.
ii) Tell the examiner whether the change was to the rhythm or to the pitch.

What the question is for:

- To develop your **musical memory.**
- To develop your **awareness of rhythm and pitch.**

Hints

- If it helps, **sing or hum** along with the piano when the melody is played the first time. When the melody is played the second time it is better just to listen for the change.
- As soon as you hear the change, let the examiner know by **raising your hand clearly and confidently.**
- For a change to the **rhythm**, the length of at least two notes will be affected.
- If you noticed one of the notes was higher or lower, you know that it is a change to the **pitch.**

Try the tests

CD1 29 - 41

Listen to the CD or ask your teacher to play the tests for you. Each track on the CD contains a complete set of questions. The answers to the tests can be found on pages 9-13 of the **Answer Booklet.**

Grade 3

About the test piece:

metre $\frac{3}{4}$ or $\frac{4}{4}$

length four bars

key major or minor

style single line melody in treble clef (or appropriate clef)

features begins with a rising interval of a major 2nd, major 3rd, perfect 4th, perfect 5th or major 6th

All questions will be based on the same piece of music.

Question 1

What the examiner will do:

Play the melody twice.

What you will be asked to do:

Clap the pulse on the second playing, stressing the strong beat.

What the question is for:

- To learn to recognise and respond to a **regular pulse.**
- To recognise whether beats are grouped in **threes or fours.**
- To recognise **where each bar begins.**

Hints

- Listen for the first beat of each bar. If each down beat (the strong first beat of the bar) is followed by **two** weak beats, then the time signature is $\frac{3}{4}$. If each down beat is followed by **three** weak beats, then the time signature is $\frac{4}{4}$.
- Remember that notes might last for more than one beat, and that more than one note might fit into one beat. Get used to the various different rhythms which can fill a bar of each time signature. Make sure that you maintain a firm and regular pulse whatever the rhythm.
- Remember to make the first beat of each bar really clear by clapping or tapping it much more loudly than the other beats. Try using a big hand movement for the strong beat, and a smaller hand movement for the weaker beats.
- Remember that the examiner will not ask you to name the time signature, but will hear your answer from the pattern of your clapping.
- You don't have to wait until the second playing to try out your clapping. The first playing is your chance to check whether the melody is in $\frac{3}{4}$ or $\frac{4}{4}$. If your strong clap isn't always on the strong beat of the bar you have the wrong time signature; try the other one. You will be marked on the second playing only, so you can try out your answer during the first playing.

Question 2

What the examiner will do:

Play the melody once.

What you will be asked to do:

Tell the examiner whether the piece is in a **major or minor key.**

What the question is for:

- To develop your skills in **recognising major and minor keys** (tonality).
- To learn the **words** to describe what you hear.

Hints

- The melody will have a **mood or feeling** and this is determined by the type of scale it is based on. You will probably already have played or sung both **major and minor scales** by now. Try to imagine the moods these scales give.
- Try singing major and minor scales before playing them on your instrument. If you can sing them, you can imagine them; if you can imagine them, you can recognise them.
- **Major** is sometimes associated with a happy or bright mood. **Minor** is sometimes associated with a sad or dull mood. Words cannot really describe major and minor accurately; you have to know how they feel.

Question 3

What the examiner will do:

Play the first two notes of the melody once.

What you will be asked to do:

Name the interval made by the first two notes of the melody. The interval will be a 2nd, 3rd, 4th, 5th or 6th.

What the question is for:

- To develop your skills in **recognising intervals** (the distance between notes).
- To learn the words to **describe** what you hear.

Hints

- An interval is the distance between two notes.
- At this grade all intervals are major or perfect, but you only need to identify them by number (**2nd, 3rd, 4th, 5th** or **6th**).
- You can get used to the sounds of intervals by thinking about each interval in scales, arpeggios and tunes that you know. Singing the interval might help you to recognise it in the exam. **Don't forget that you can sing or hum the notes before you answer in the exam** if you want to.
- You can find intervals of a 2nd, 3rd, 4th, 5th and 6th by singing up a major scale, counting from the first note:

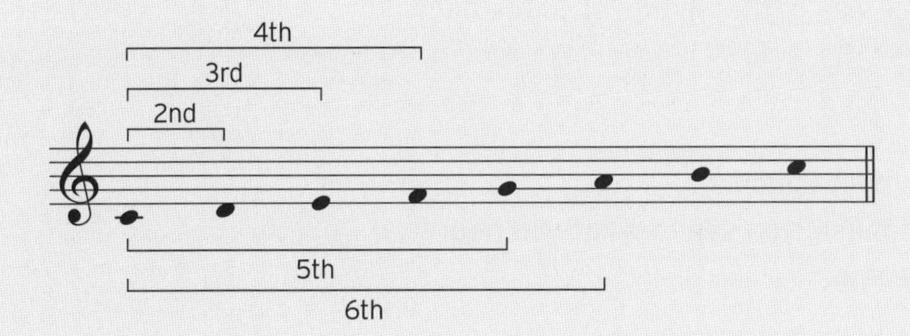

- You can find intervals of a 3rd, 4th and 5th in major arpeggios:

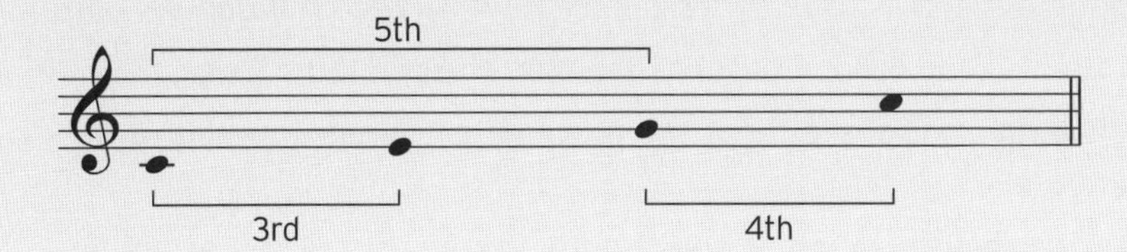

- Here are some tunes which start with these intervals. Try to find some others.

(Major) 2nd

Congratulations
Frère Jacques
Happy Birthday (second and third notes)
Rudolph the Red-nosed Reindeer
Silent Night

(Major) 3rd

Morning Has Broken
Oh, when the Saints
Once in Royal David's City
Pop Goes the Weasel
While Shepherds Watched their Flocks by Night

(Perfect) 4th

Amazing Grace
Auld Lang Syne
If You're Happy and You Know It (second and third notes)
We Wish You a Merry Christmas
Wedding March (Bridal Chorus from *Lohengrin*)

(Perfect) 5th

Also Sprach Zarathustra (*2001: A Space Odyssey* theme)
Baa Baa Black Sheep (second and third notes)
Scarborough Fair (second and third notes)
Star Wars theme
Twinkle, Twinkle, Little Star (second and third notes)

(Major 6th)

Crimond
Dashing through the Snow
For He's a Jolly Good Fellow
Hush, Little Baby
My Bonnie Lies Over the Ocean

- The intervals for this test will always be played from low note to high note (ie ascending).

Question 4

What the examiner will do:

- Give you a printed copy of the melody.
- Play the melody twice, first as printed and then with one change to the rhythm or to the pitch.

What you will be asked to do:

i) Identify the bar in which the change took place.
ii) Tell the examiner whether the change was to the rhythm or to the pitch.

What the question is for:

- To develop your **musical memory.**
- To develop your **awareness of rhythm and pitch.**
- To develop your skills in **relating the music you see to what you hear.**
- To improve the **accuracy of your reading.**

Hints

- You will already have heard the original version **four times** before hearing the changed version.
- Try to concentrate on listening to the melody while you are following the printed music.
- Concentrate on the shape of the melody and look out for the place where what you hear does not match what you are looking at.
- Either use the printed copy to point to the bar in which the change occurs, or tell the examiner the bar number where the change occurs.
- Remember that **you are not allowed to make any marks on the copy of the music** you have been given, **or make any other notes during the test**. Get used to remembering where the change was, or point to the change with your finger.
- If you play an instrument that usually uses bass or alto clef you can **ask for a copy of the melody in the clef you normally use.**

Try the tests

CD2 01 - 10

Listen to the CD or ask your teacher to play the tests for you. Each track on the CD contains a complete set of questions. The answers to the tests can be found on pages 14-17 of the **Answer Booklet**.

Printed below is the music you need for Question 4 of each set. Don't look at the music until you reach Question 4.

If you want to practise Question 4 using bass or alto clef, copies of the melodies can be downloaded from www.trinitycollege.com/music

Music for Grade 3 Question 4

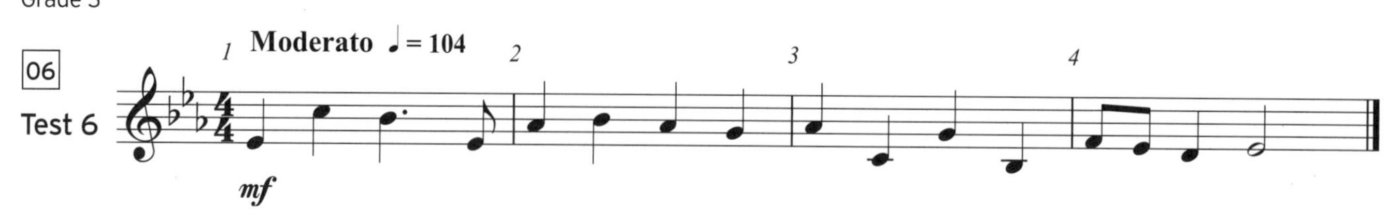
06
Test 6
Moderato ♩ = 104
1
2
3
4
mf

07
Test 7
Moderato ♩ = 104
1
2
3
4
mf

08
Test 8
Moderato ♩ = 104
1
2
3
4
mf

09
Test 9
Moderato ♩ = 104
1
2
3
4
mf

10
Test 10
Moderato ♩ = 104
1
2
3
4
mf

Aural Book 1

Answer Booklet

for Trinity College London exams from 2017

Initial–Grade 5

Published by
Trinity College London Press
trinitycollege.com

Registered in England
Company no. 09726123

Second impression, June 2017

Printed in England by Caligraving Ltd.

Introduction

This booklet is intended to be used:

either in conjunction with the CDs and the book **Aural 1** to check and mark candidates' answers
or by teachers or others delivering the sample tests at the piano (or other instruments).

It includes all the text and music heard on the CDs.

The first test in each grade shows how the answers are notated for all subsequent questions. No specialist knowledge is required to use this feature, making it possible for any parent or helper to assist with preparation by checking the candidate's answers.

Contents

Initial

Question 1
I am going to play a melody three times. Listen twice, then join in from the start of the third playing, clapping the pulse and stressing the strong beat. **[Play the melody twice and then say 'Now join in']**

Question 2
Listen again, then tell me if it was *forte* or *piano*. **[Play melody]**

Question 3
Listen again, then tell me if it was *legato* or *staccato*. **[Play melody]**

Question 4
Now, listen to the first three notes of the melody, then tell me which was the highest (or lowest). **[Play first three notes]**

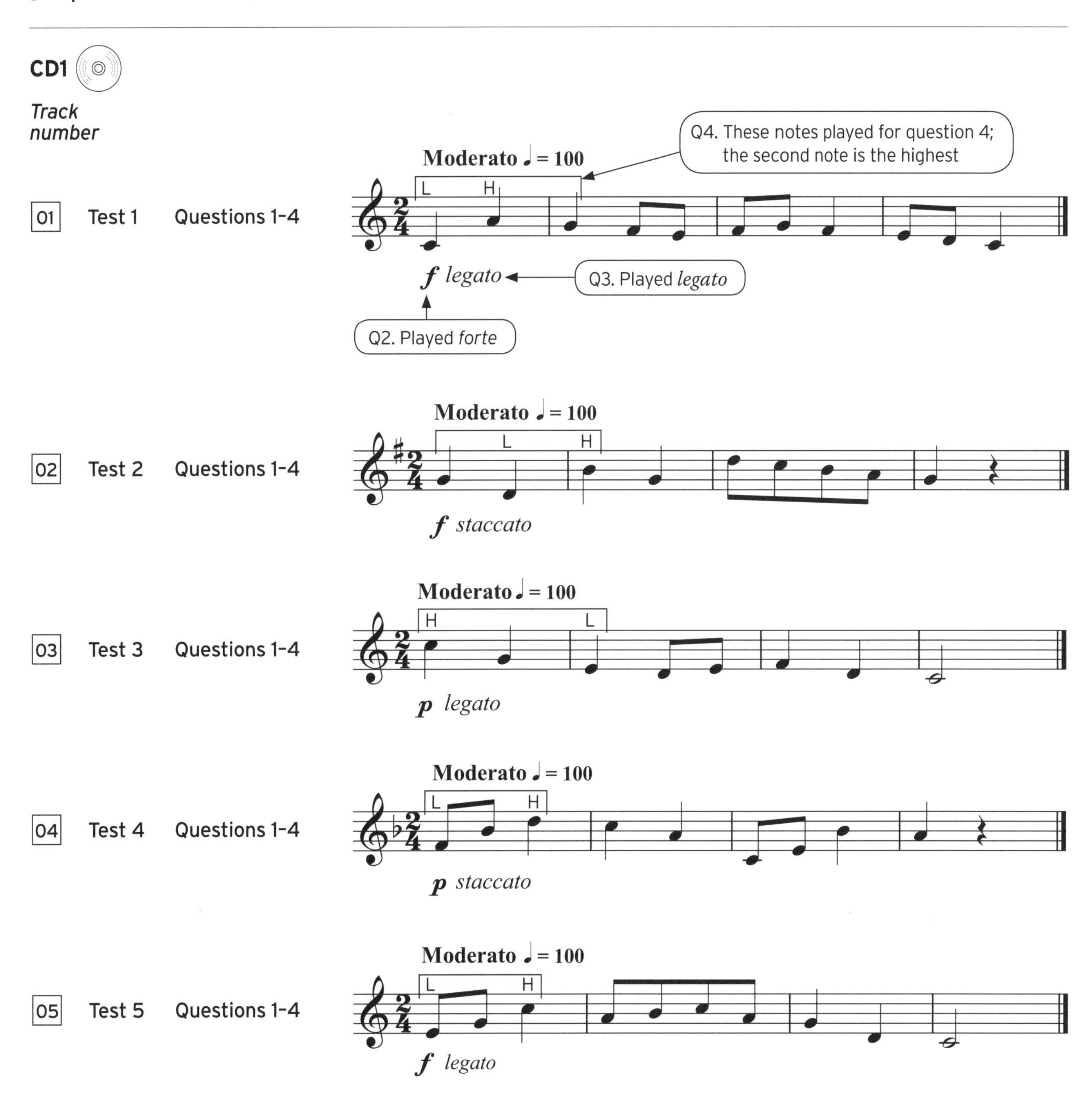

06 Test 6 Questions 1–4
Moderato ♩ = 100
L H
p staccato
07 Test 7 Questions 1–4
Moderato ♩ = 100
L H
f legato
08 Test 8 Questions 1–4
Moderato ♩ = 100
L H
f staccato
09 Test 9 Questions 1–4
Moderato ♩ = 100
L H
p legato
10 Test 10 Questions 1–4
Moderato ♩ = 100
L H
f legato
11 Test 11 Questions 1–4
Moderato ♩ = 100
L H
f staccato
12 Test 12 Questions 1–4
Moderato ♩ = 100
L H
p staccato
13 Test 13 Questions 1–4
Moderato ♩ = 100
L H
p legato
14 Test 14 Questions 1–4
Moderato ♩ = 100
H L
f legato

Grade 1

Question 1
I am going to play a melody three times. Listen twice, then join in from the start of the third playing, clapping the pulse and stressing the strong beat. **[Play the melody twice and then say 'Now join in']**

Question 2
Listen again, then tell me if it was *forte* or *piano*, and *legato* or *staccato*. **[Play melody]**

Question 3
Listen to the first two bars, then tell me if the last note was higher or lower than the first note.
[Play first two bars of melody]

Question 4
Now, I am going to play the melody twice more. The second playing will have one change. Please raise your hand when you hear the change.* Here is the melody for the first time. **[Play original melody once]**
Now with the change. **[Play the changed version of the melody]**

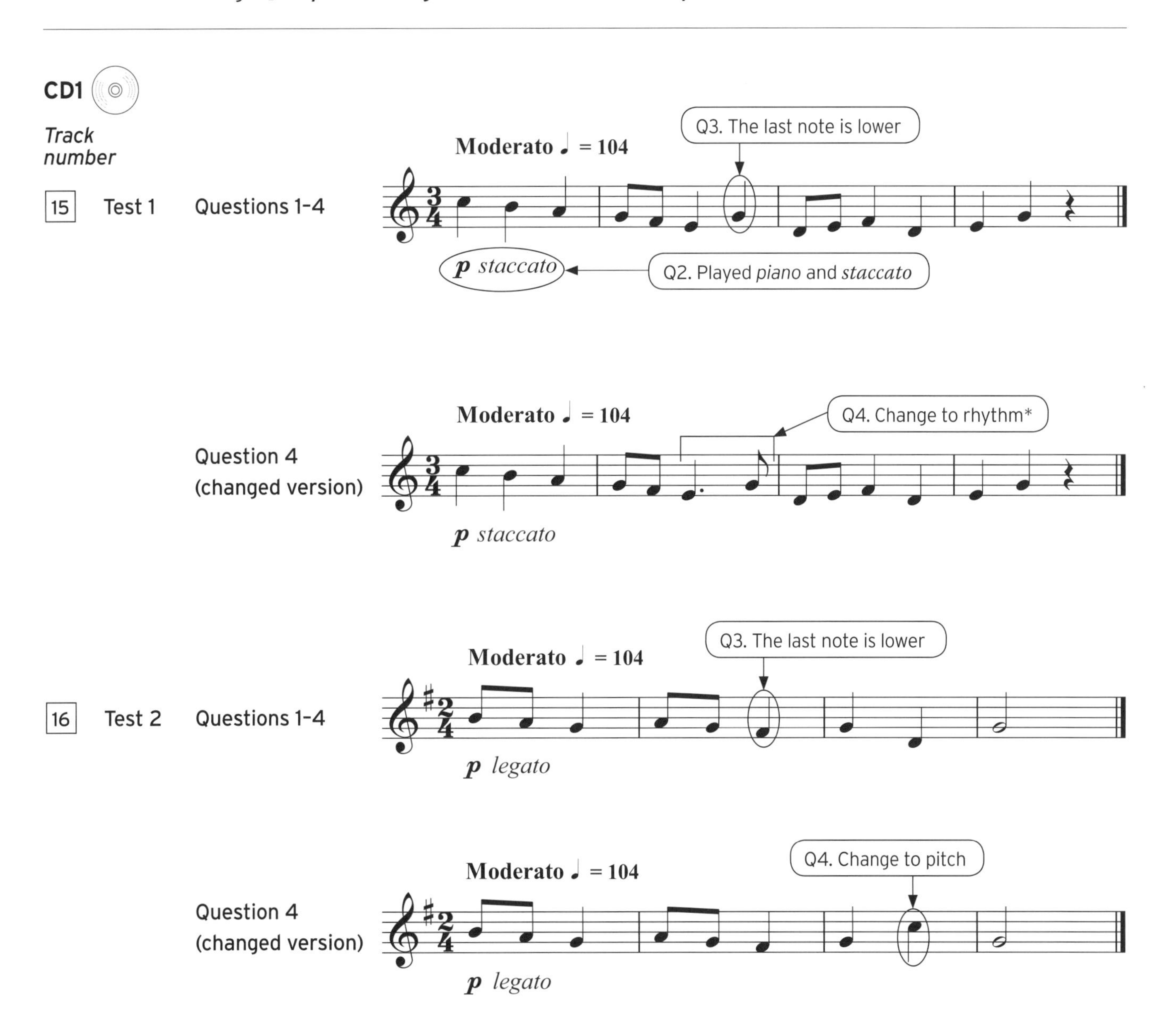

* At Grade 1 candidates are not required to identify the type of change.

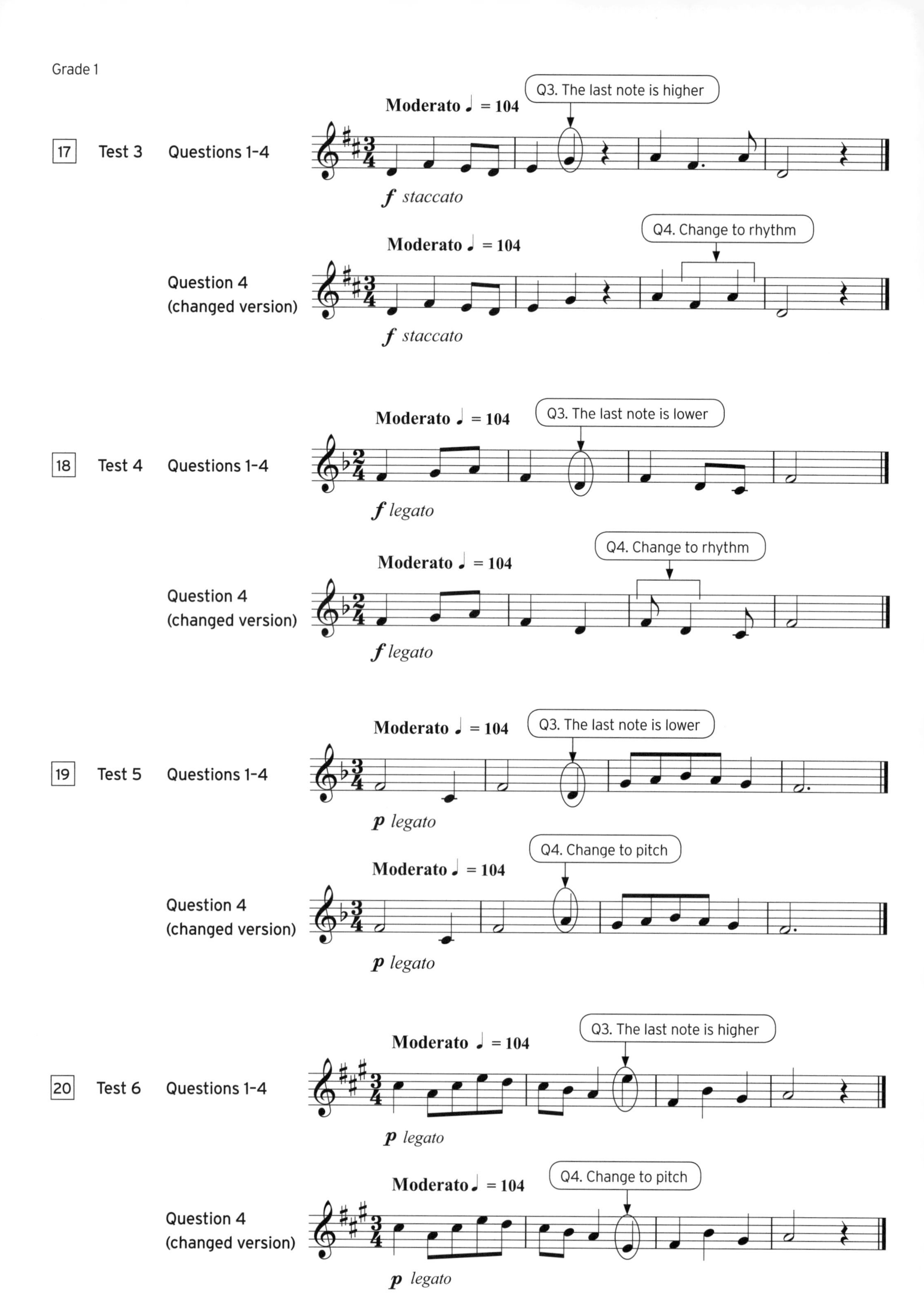
17
Test 3
Questions 1-4
Moderato ♩ = 104
Q3. The last note is higher
f staccato
Question 4
(changed version)
Moderato ♩ = 104
Q4. Change to rhythm
f staccato
18
Test 4
Questions 1-4
Moderato ♩ = 104
Q3. The last note is lower
f legato
Question 4
(changed version)
Moderato ♩ = 104
Q4. Change to rhythm
f legato
19
Test 5
Questions 1-4
Moderato ♩ = 104
Q3. The last note is lower
p legato
Question 4
(changed version)
Moderato ♩ = 104
Q4. Change to pitch
p legato
20
Test 6
Questions 1-4
Moderato ♩ = 104
Q3. The last note is higher
p legato
Question 4
(changed version)
Moderato ♩ = 104
Q4. Change to pitch
p legato

21
Test 7
Questions 1-4
Moderato ♩ = 104
Q3. The last note is lower
f staccato
Question 4
(changed version)
Moderato ♩ = 104
Q4. Change to rhythm
f staccato
22
Test 8
Questions 1-4
Moderato ♩ = 104
Q3. The last note is higher
p legato
Question 4
(changed version)
Moderato ♩ = 104
Q4. Change to pitch
p legato
23
Test 9
Questions 1-4
Moderato ♩ = 104
Q3. The last note is lower
f staccato
Question 4
(changed version)
Moderato ♩ = 104
Q4. Change to rhythm
f staccato
24
Test 10
Questions 1-4
Moderato ♩ = 104
Q3. The last note is higher
f legato
Question 4
(changed version)
Moderato ♩ = 104
Q4. Change to rhythm
f legato

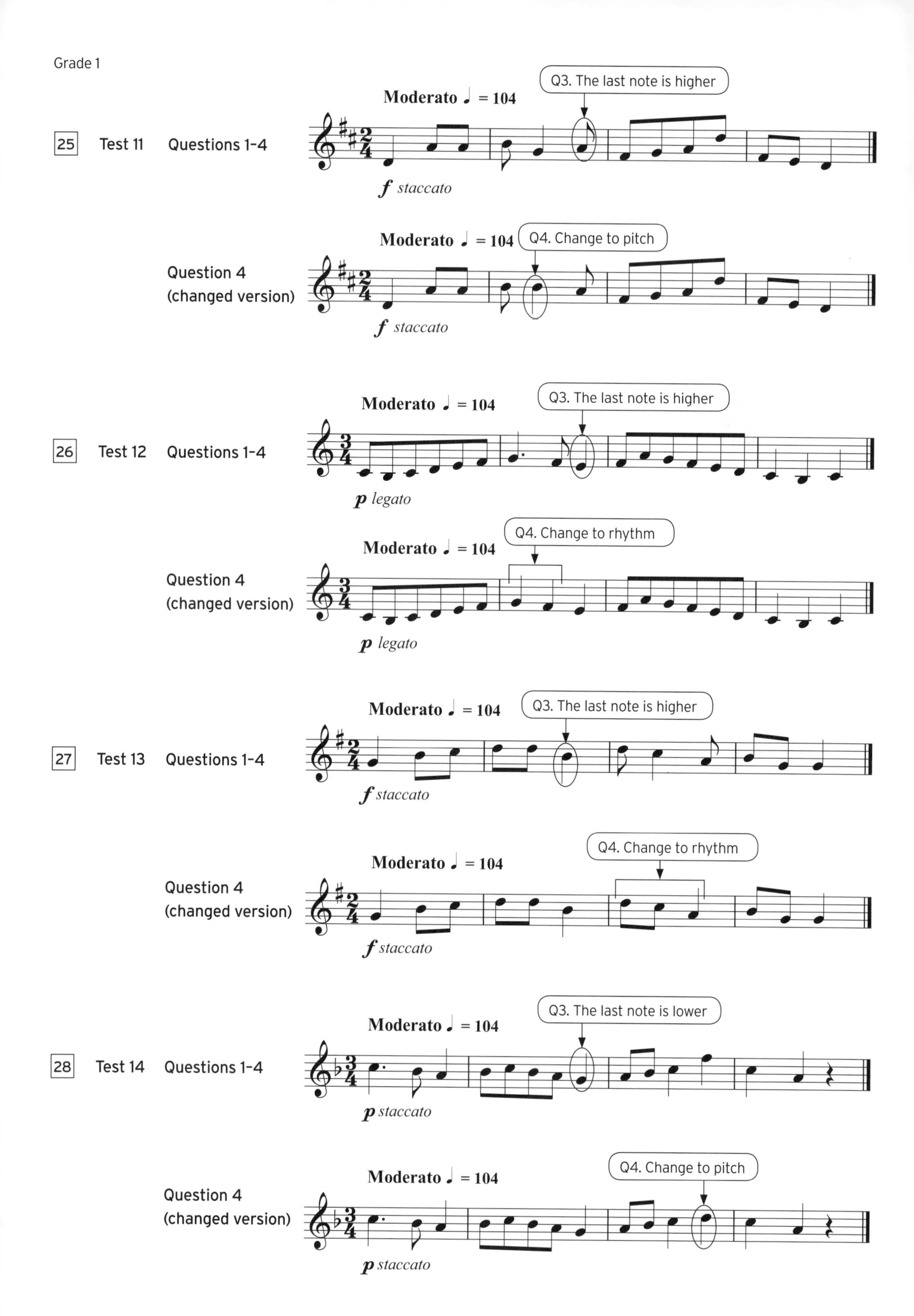
25
Test 11
Questions 1-4
Moderato ♩ = 104
Q3. The last note is higher
f staccato
Question 4
(changed version)
Moderato ♩ = 104
Q4. Change to pitch
f staccato
26
Test 12
Questions 1-4
Moderato ♩ = 104
Q3. The last note is higher
p legato
Question 4
(changed version)
Moderato ♩ = 104
Q4. Change to rhythm
p legato
27
Test 13
Questions 1-4
Moderato ♩ = 104
Q3. The last note is higher
f staccato
Question 4
(changed version)
Moderato ♩ = 104
Q4. Change to rhythm
f staccato
28
Test 14
Questions 1-4
Moderato ♩ = 104
Q3. The last note is lower
p staccato
Question 4
(changed version)
Moderato ♩ = 104
Q4. Change to pitch
p staccato

Grade 2

Question 1
I am going to play a melody three times. Listen twice, then join in from the start of the third playing, clapping the pulse and stressing the strong beat. **[Play the melody twice and then say 'Now join in']**

Question 2
Listen again, then tell me about the dynamics, and whether it was *legato* or *staccato*. **[Play melody]**

Question 3
Listen again, then tell me if the last note was higher or lower than the first note. **[Play melody]**

Question 4
Now, I am going to play the melody twice more. The second playing will have one change. Please raise your hand when you hear the change, then tell me whether it was a change in pitch or rhythm. Here is the melody for the first time. **[Play original melody once]** Now with the change. **[Play the changed version of the melody]**

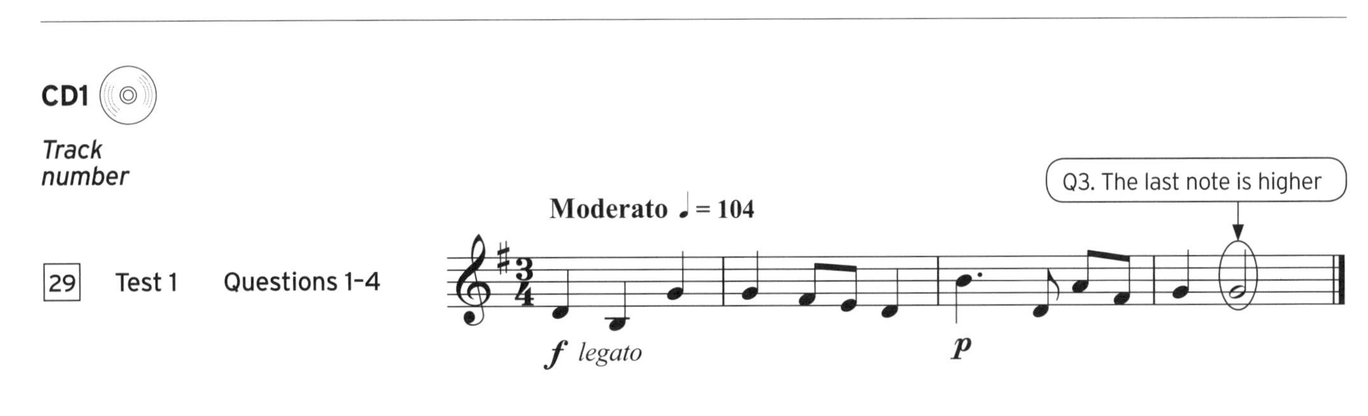

Question 2 The melody started *forte* and ended *piano*. It was played *legato*.

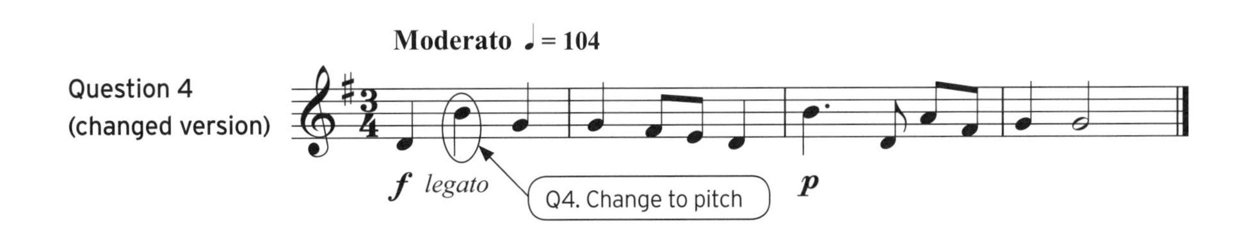

30 Test 2 Questions 1–4

Question 2 The melody started *piano* and ended *forte*. It was played *staccato*.

Question 4 (changed version)

31 Test 3 Questions 1–4

Question 2 The melody started *piano* and ended *forte*. It was played *legato*.

Question 4 (changed version)

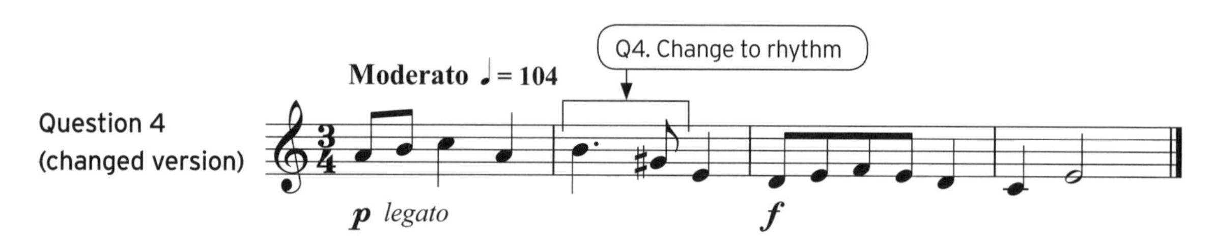

32 Test 4 Questions 1–4

Question 2 The melody started *forte* and ended *piano*. It was played *legato*.

Question 4 (changed version)

33 **Test 5** **Questions 1–4**

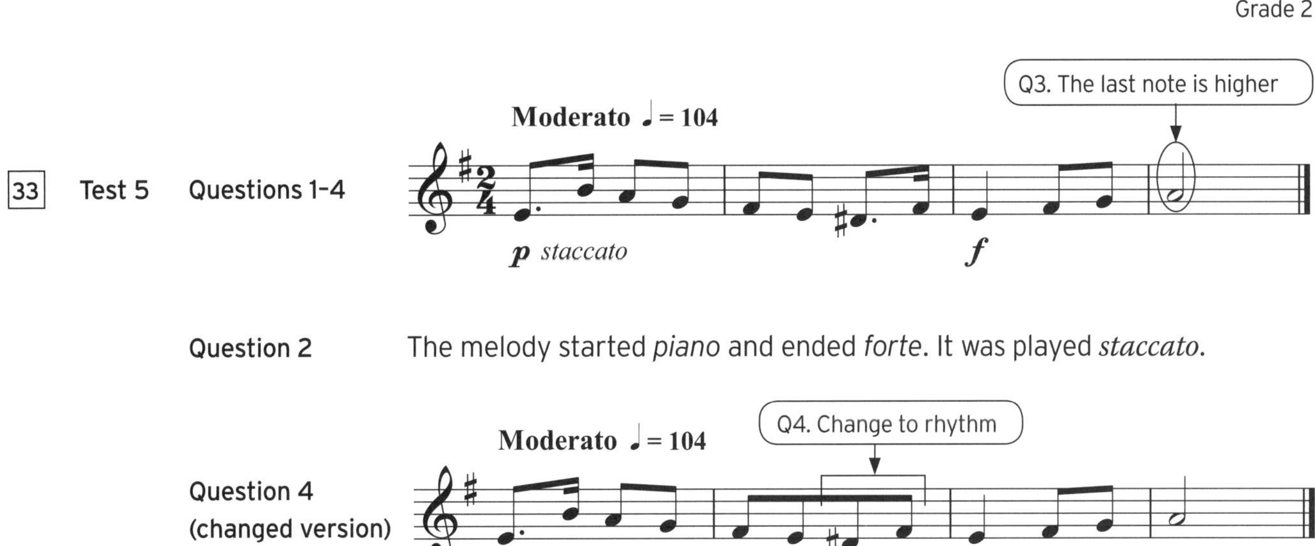

Question 2 The melody started *piano* and ended *forte*. It was played *staccato*.

Question 4 (changed version)

34 **Test 6** **Questions 1–4**

Question 2 The melody started *forte* and ended *piano*. It was played *legato*.

Question 4 (changed version)

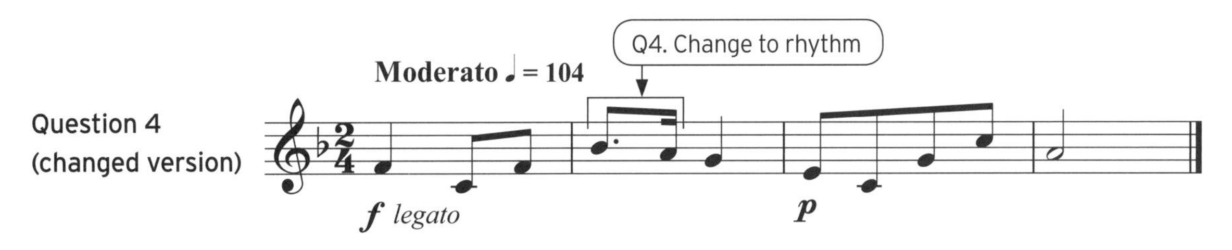

35 **Test 7** **Questions 1–4**

Question 2 The melody started *piano* and ended *forte*. It was played *legato*.

Question 4 (changed version)

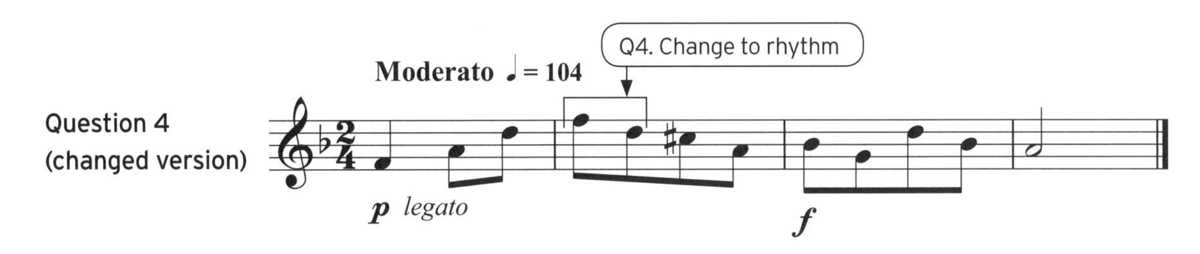

Question 2 The melody started *piano* and ended *forte*. It was played *legato*.

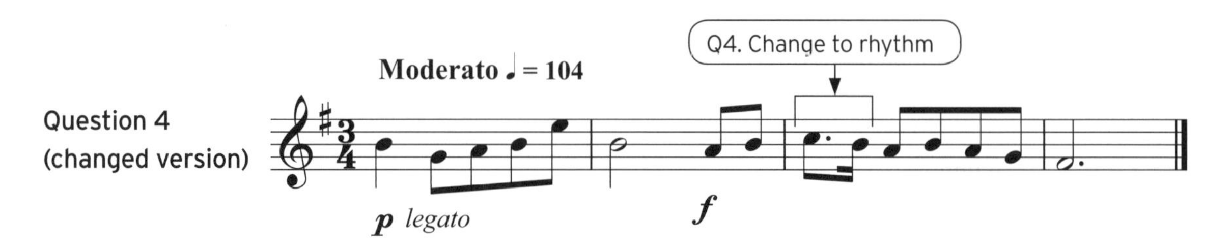

Question 2 The melody started *forte* and ended *piano*. It was played *staccato*.

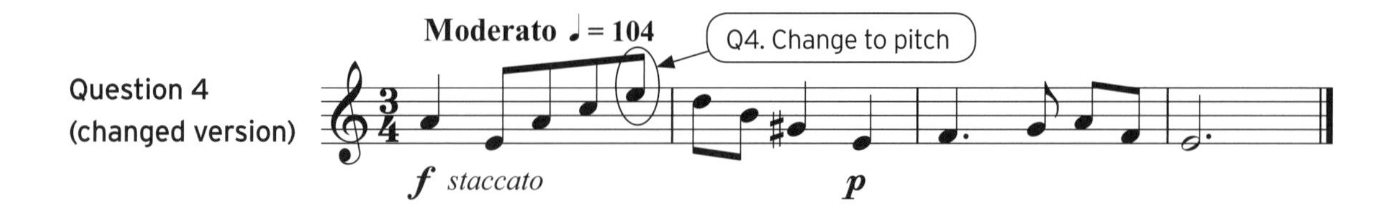

Question 2 The melody started *forte* and ended *piano*. It was played *legato*.

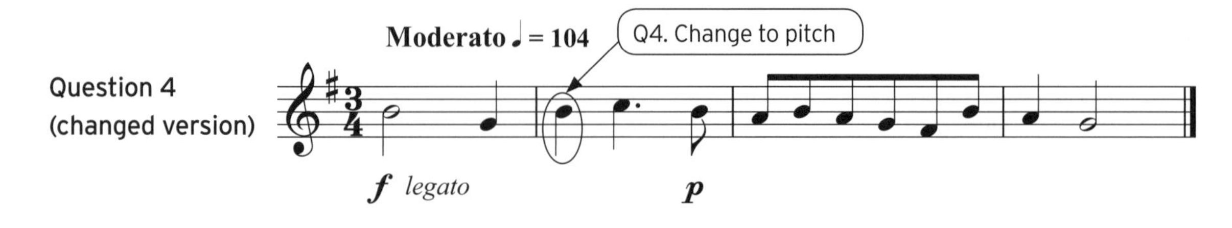

39 **Test 11** **Questions 1–4**

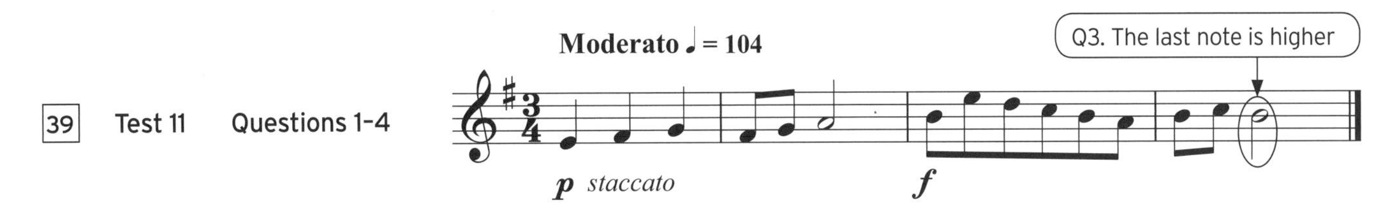

Question 2 The melody started *piano* and ended *forte*. It was played *staccato*.

Question 4 (changed version)

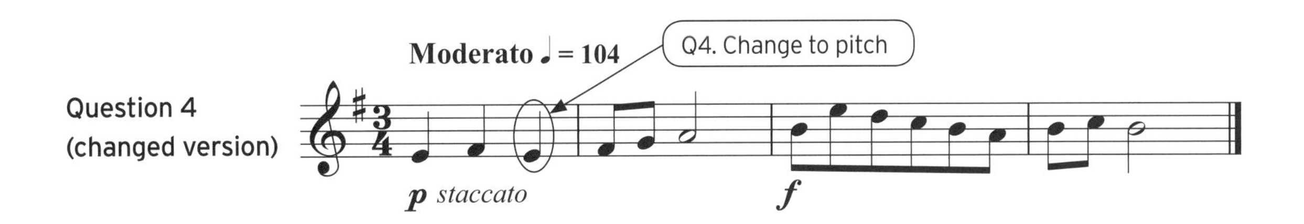

40 **Test 12** **Questions 1–4**

Question 2 The melody started *forte* and ended *piano*. It was played *staccato*.

Question 4 (changed version)

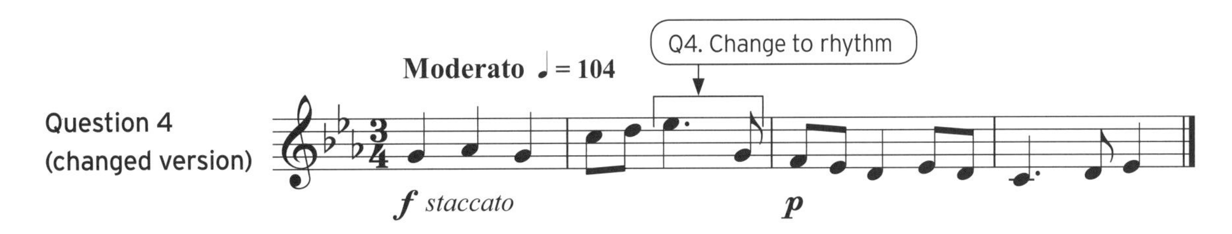

41 **Test 13** **Questions 1–4**

Question 2 The melody started *forte* and ended *piano*. It was played *staccato*.

Question 4 (changed version)

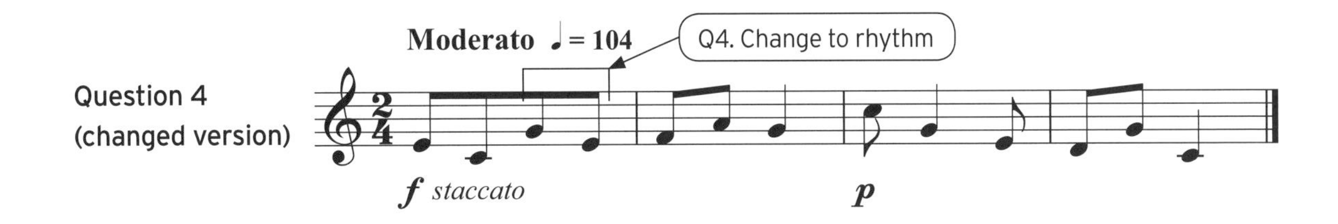

Grade 3

Question 1
I am going to play a melody twice. Listen, then join in from the start of the second playing, clapping the pulse and stressing the strong beat. **[Play the melody once and then say 'Now join in']**

Question 2
Listen again, then tell me if it was major or minor. **[Play melody]**

Question 3
Listen to the first two notes of the melody, then tell me the interval.* **[Play first two notes of melody consecutively, holding the lower while playing the higher]**

Question 4
Here is a copy of the melody. I am going to play it twice more. The second playing will have one change. Tell me or show me in which bar the change happened and if it was pitch or rhythm. Here is the melody for the first time. **[Play original melody once]** Now with the change. **[Play the changed version of the melody]**

CD2

Track number

01

Test 1 Questions 1–4

Question 4 (changed version)

* At Grade 3 candidates are required to identify the interval by number only.

02

Test 2 Questions 1–4

Question 4 (changed version)

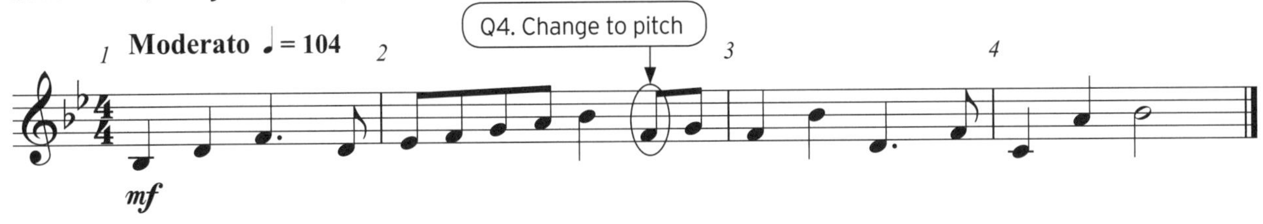

03

Test 3 Questions 1–4

Question 4 (changed version)

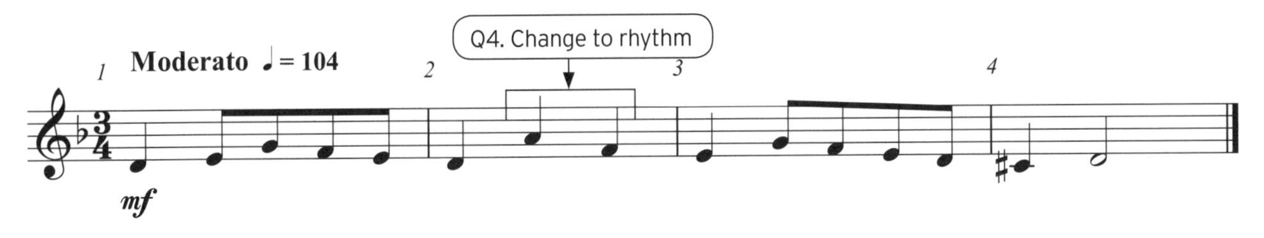

04

Test 4 Questions 1–4

Question 4 (changed version)

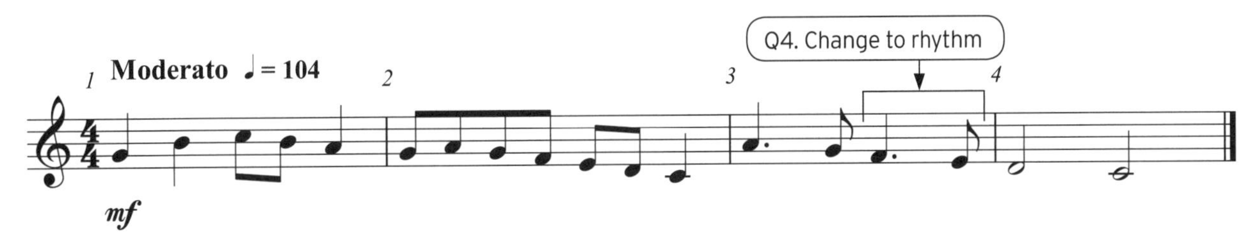

Test 5 Questions 1–4

Question 4 (changed version)

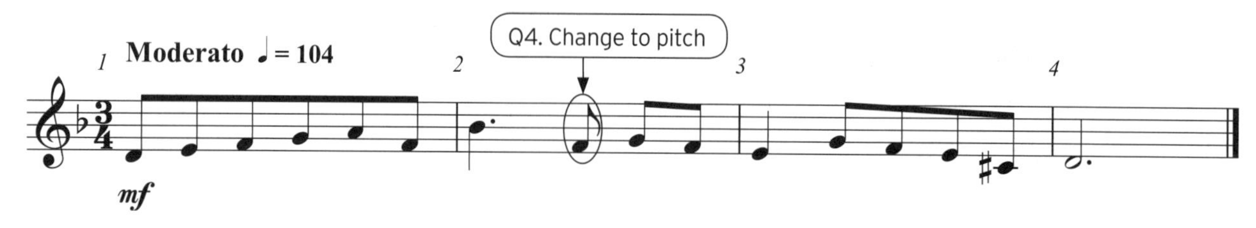

06

Test 6 Questions 1–4

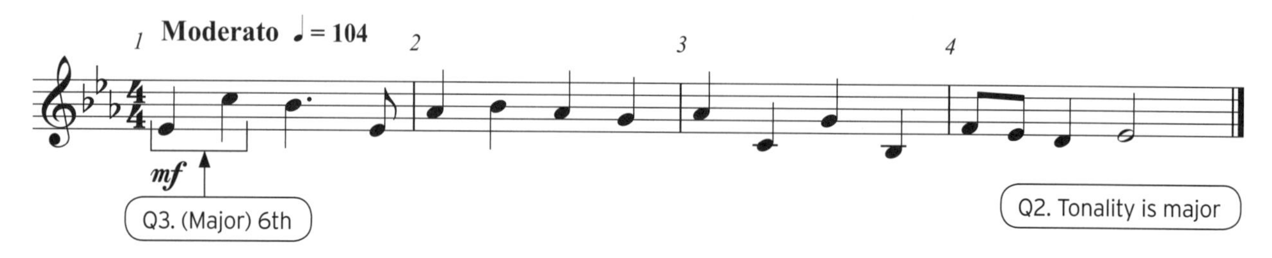

Question 4 (changed version)

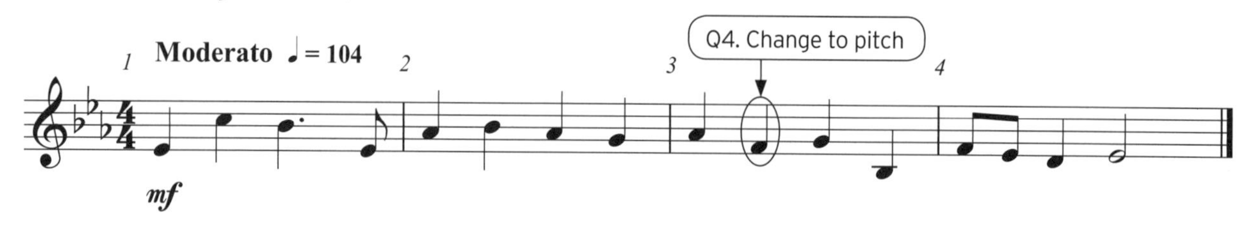

07

Test 7 Questions 1–4

Question 4 (changed version)

08

Test 8 Questions 1–4

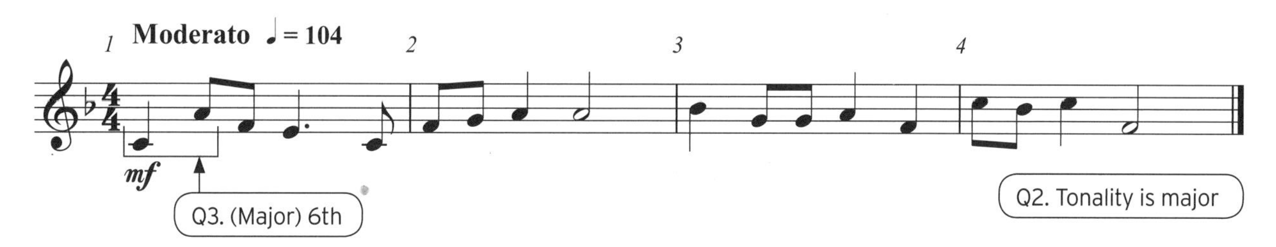

Question 4 (changed version)

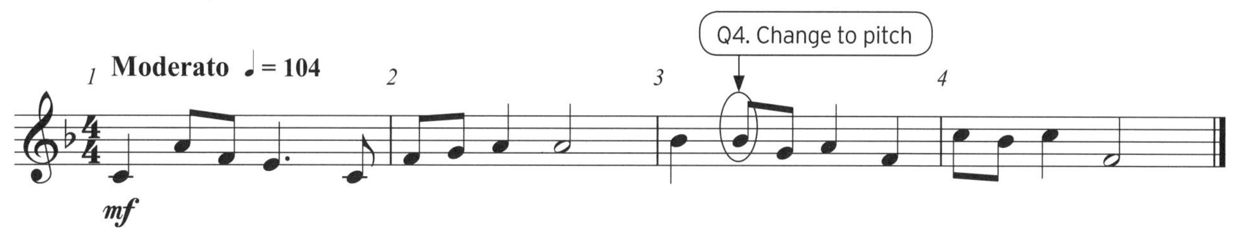

09

Test 9 Questions 1–4

Question 4 (changed version)

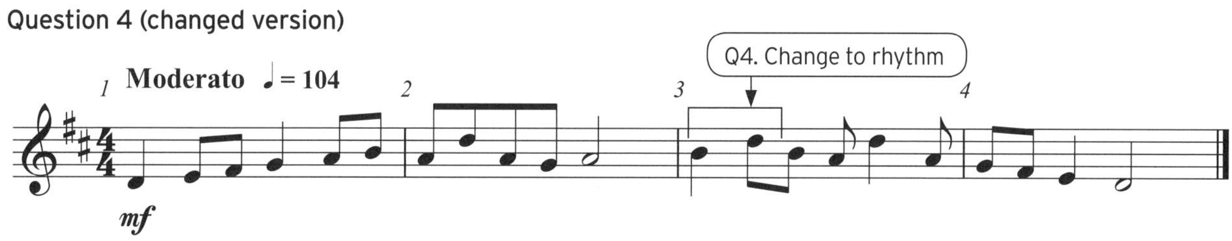

10

Test 10 Questions 1–4

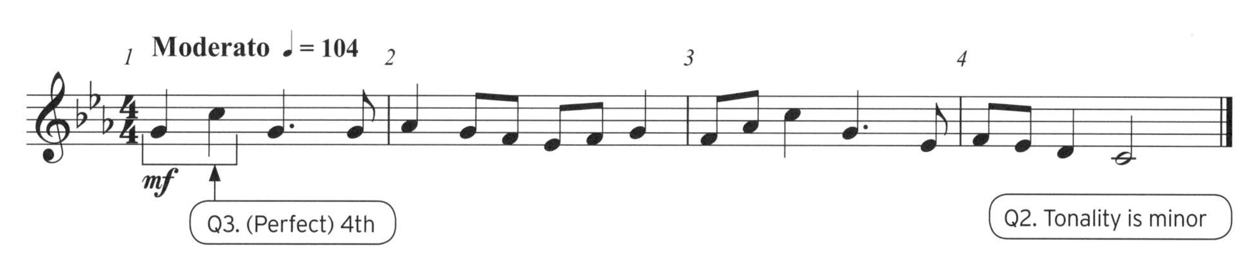

Question 4 (changed version)

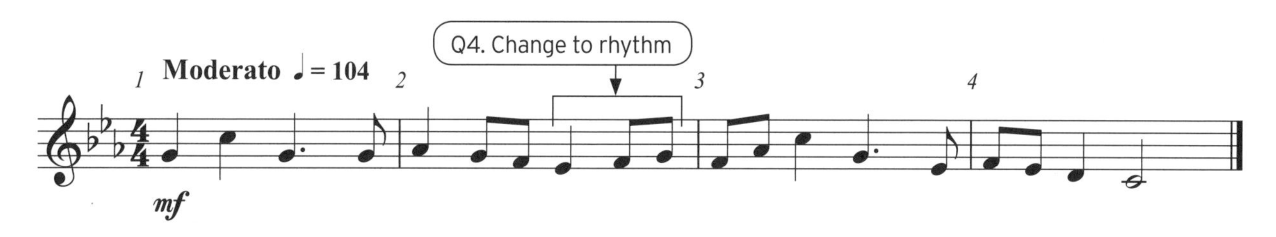

Grade 4

Question 1

I am going to play a piece twice. Listen, then join in from the start of the second playing, clapping the pulse and stressing the strong beat. **[Play the piece once and then say 'Now join in']**

Question 2

I am going to play the piece twice more. Listen, then tell me whether it was major or minor, and also name the final cadence. **[Play piece twice]**

Question 3

Now, listen to the first two notes and tell me the full name of the interval. **[Play first two notes of melody consecutively, holding the lower while playing the higher]**

Question 4

Here is a copy of the melody. I am going to play it twice more. The second playing will have two changes, one of pitch and one of rhythm. Tell me or show me in which bars the changes happened and what they were. Here is the melody for the first time. **[Play original melody once]** Now with the changes. **[Play the changed version of the melody]**

CD2 

Track number

11

Test 1 Questions 1–4 (NB only the melody line is played for Question 4)

Question 4 (changed version)

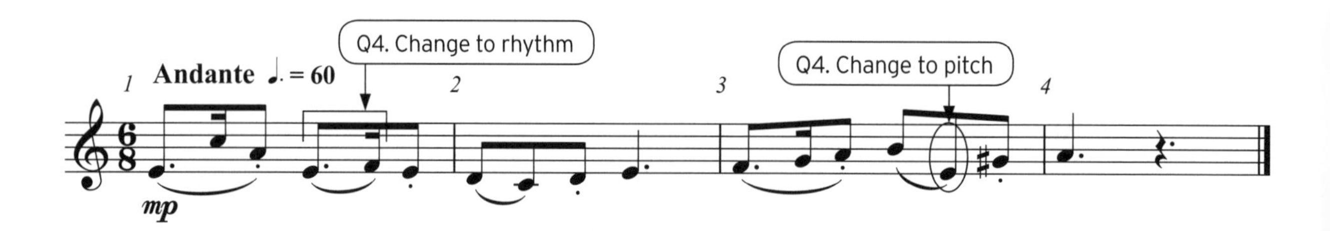

12

Test 2 Questions 1–4

Question 4 (changed version)

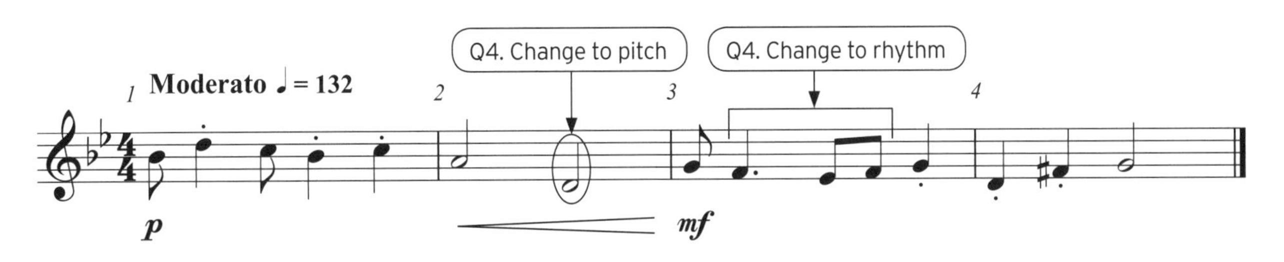

13

Test 3 Questions 1–4

Question 4 (changed version)

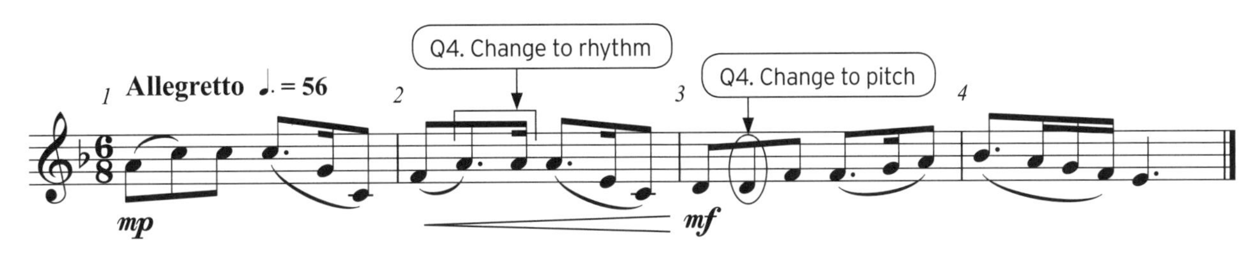

14

Test 4 Questions 1–4

Q2. Tonality is minor; Imperfect cadence

Question 4 (changed version)

15

Test 5 Questions 1–4

Q2. Tonality is major; Perfect cadence

Question 4 (changed version)

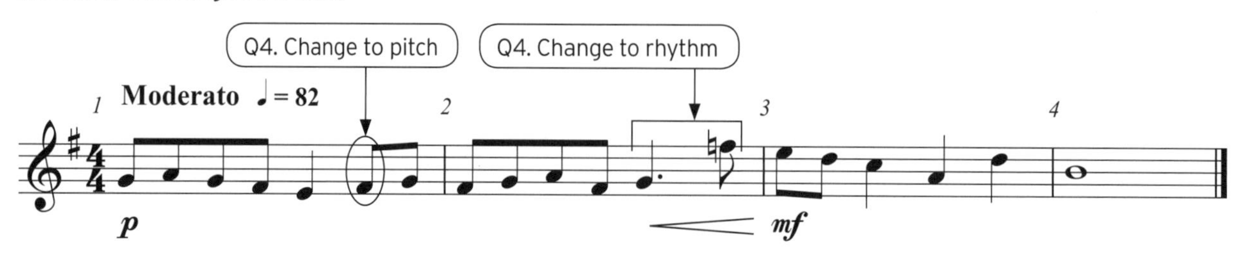

16

Test 6 Questions 1–4

Question 4 (changed version)

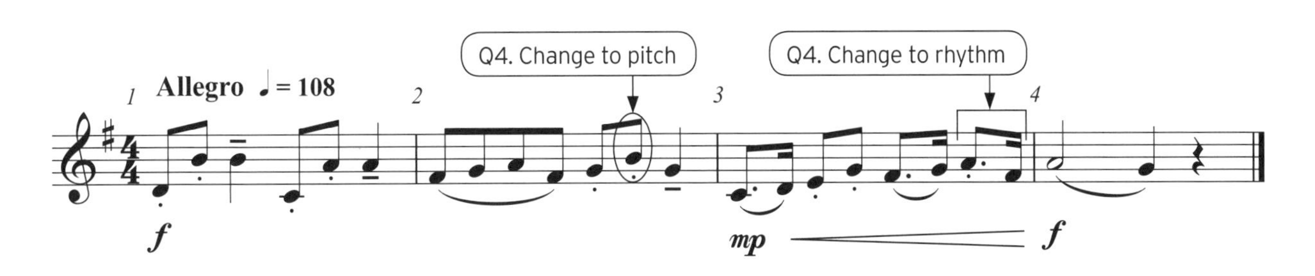

17

Test 7 Questions 1–4

Question 4 (changed version)

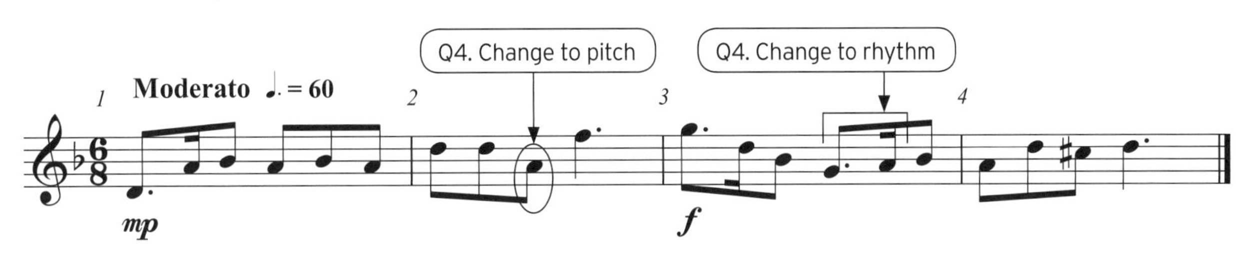

18

Test 8 Questions 1–4

Question 4 (changed version)

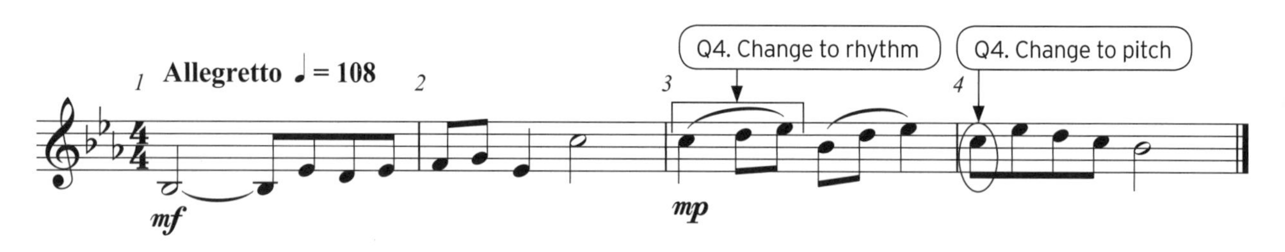

19

Test 9 Questions 1–4

Question 4 (changed version)

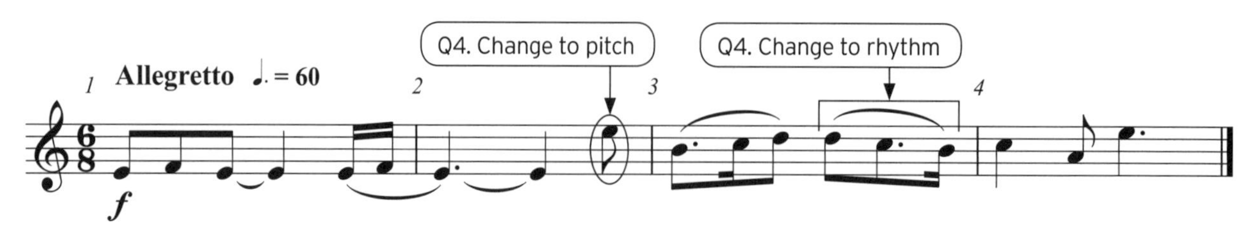

Grade 5

Question 1
I am going to play a piece twice. Listen, then join in from the start of the second playing, clapping the pulse and stressing the strong beat. Then, tell me the time signature. **[Play the piece once and then say 'Now join in']**

Question 2
I am going to play the piece twice more. Listen, then tell me about the changing tonality and also name the final cadence. **[Play piece twice]**

Question 3
Now, listen to these two notes and tell me the full name of the interval. **[Play indicated notes of melody consecutively, holding the lower while playing the higher]**

Question 4
Here is a copy of the piece. I am going to play it twice more. The second playing will have two changes to the top line, one of pitch and one of rhythm. Tell me or show me in which bars the changes happened and what they were. Here is the piece for the first time. **[Play original piece once]** Now with the changes. **[Play the changed version of the piece]**

CD2 

Track number

20

Test 1 Questions 1–4

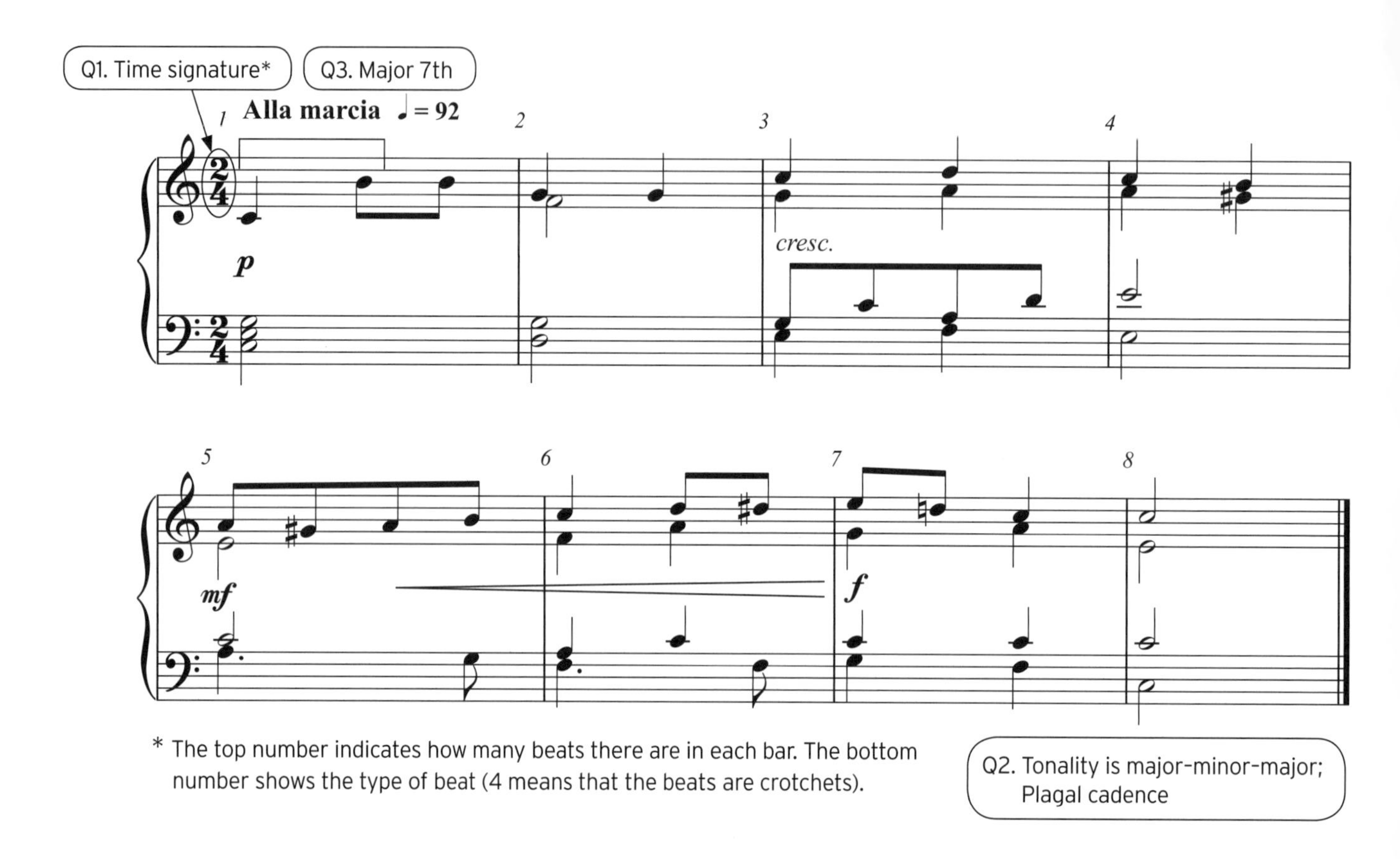

* The top number indicates how many beats there are in each bar. The bottom number shows the type of beat (4 means that the beats are crotchets).

Question 4 (changed version)

21

Test 2 Questions 1–4

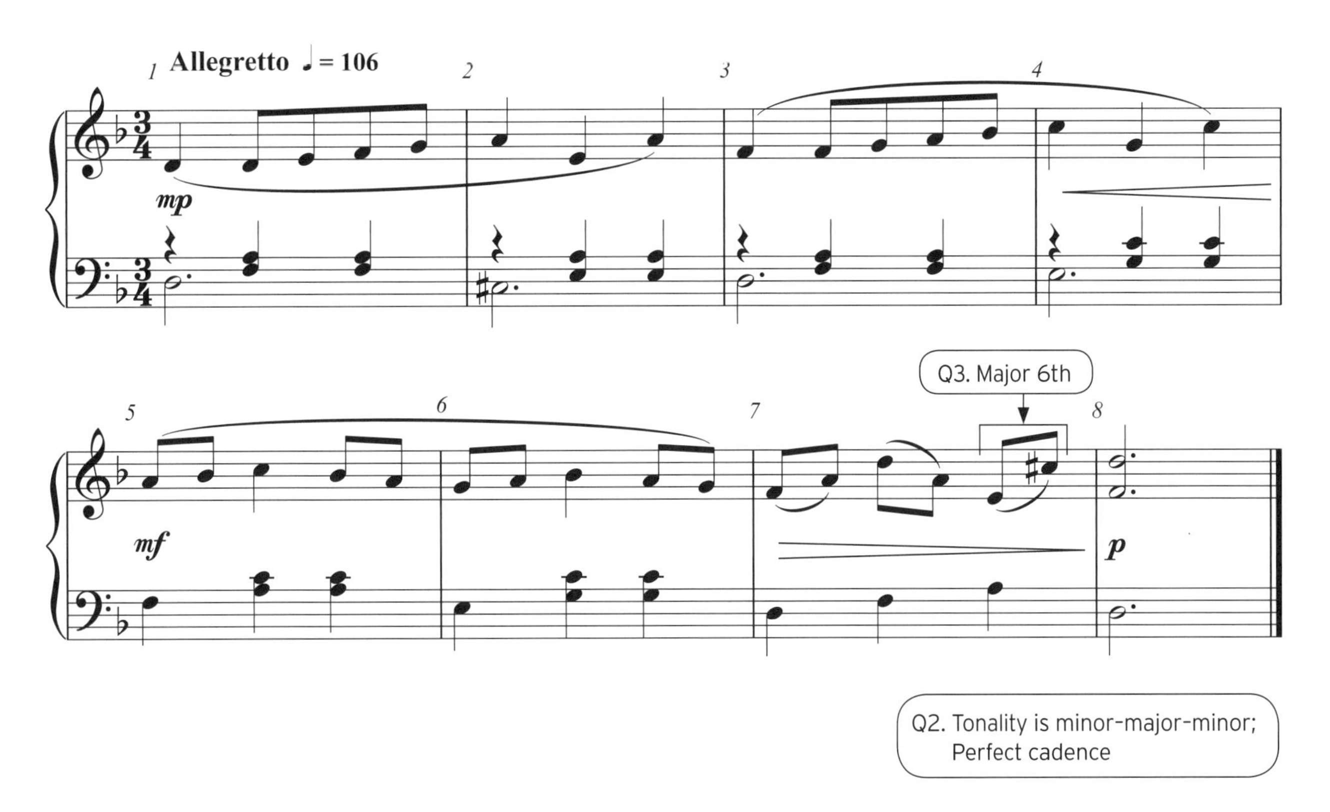

Question 4 (changed version)

22

Test 3 Questions 1–4

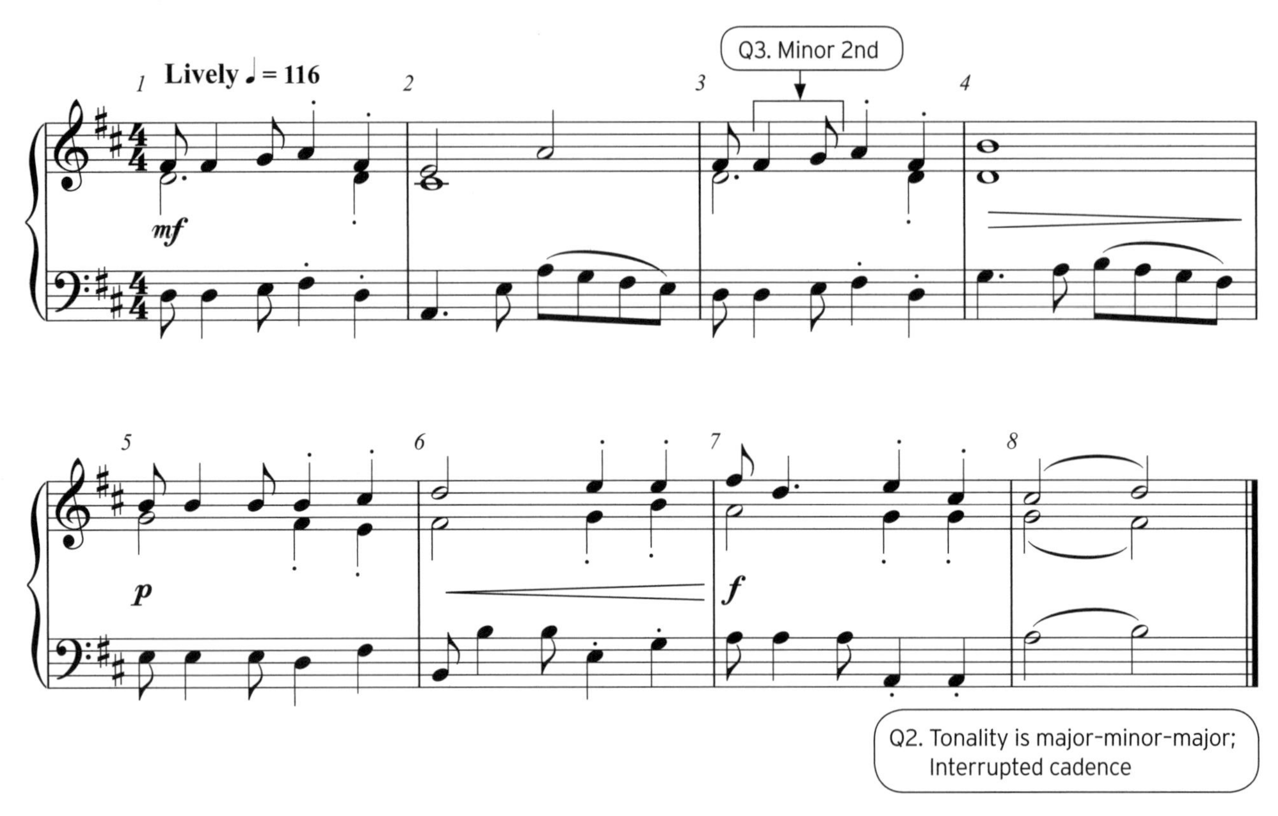

Question 4 (changed version)

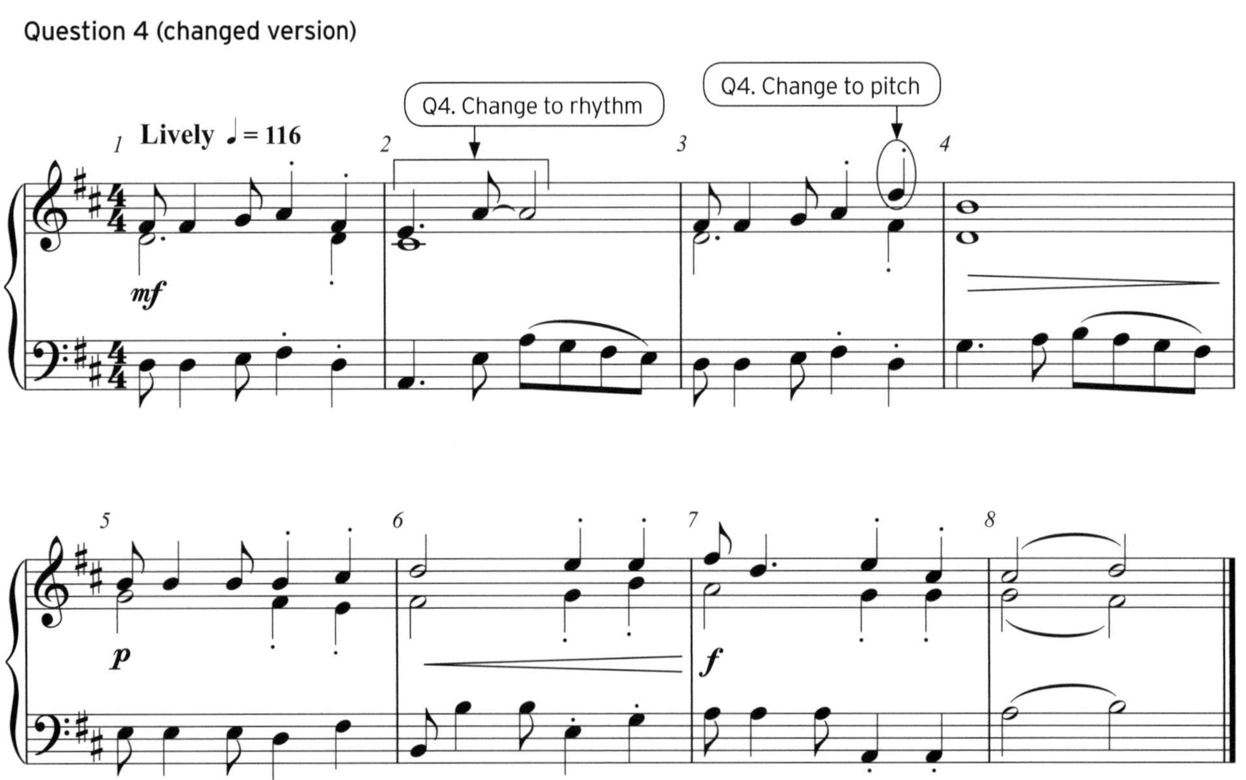

23

Test 4 Questions 1–4

Question 4 (changed version)

Test 5 Questions 1–4

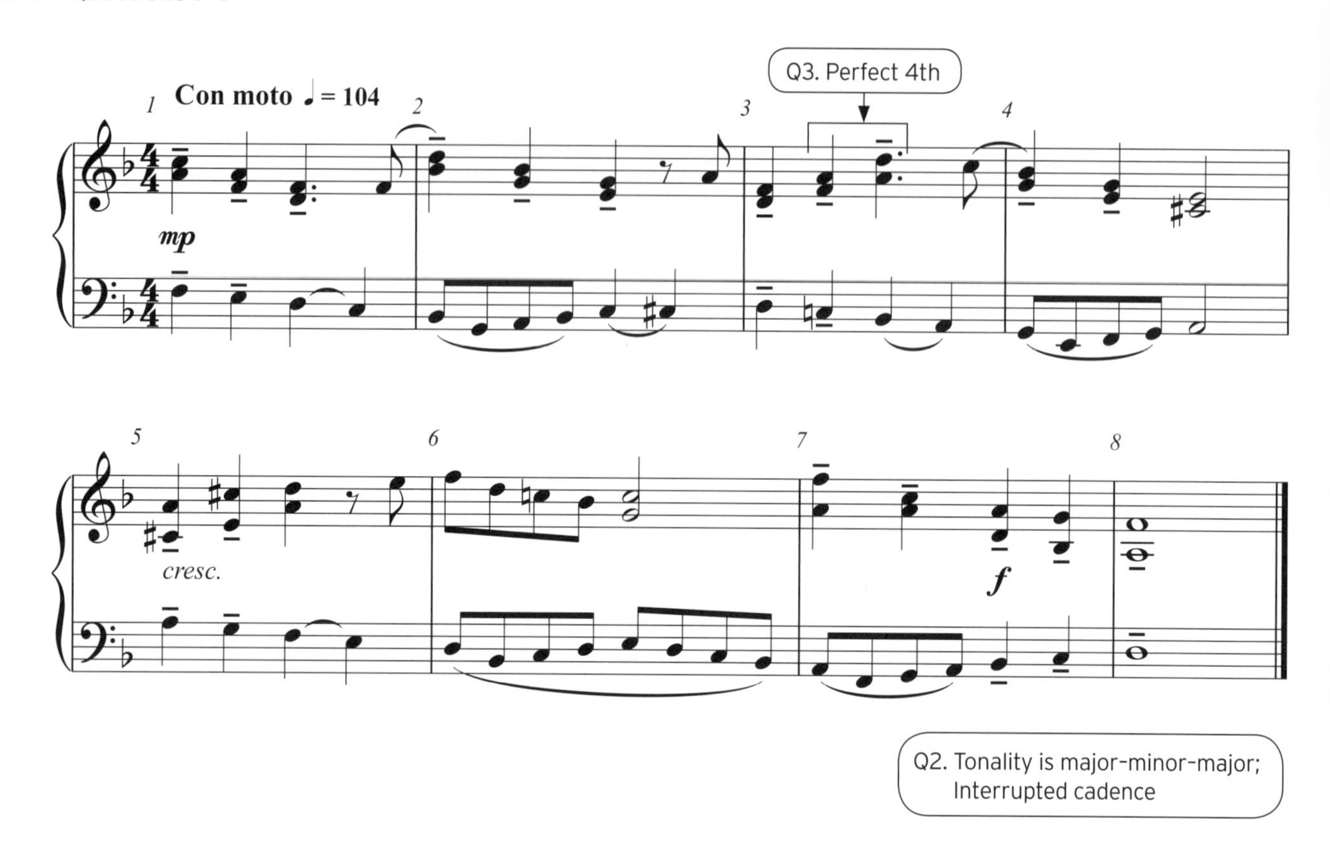

Question 4 (changed version)

25

Test 6 Questions 1–4

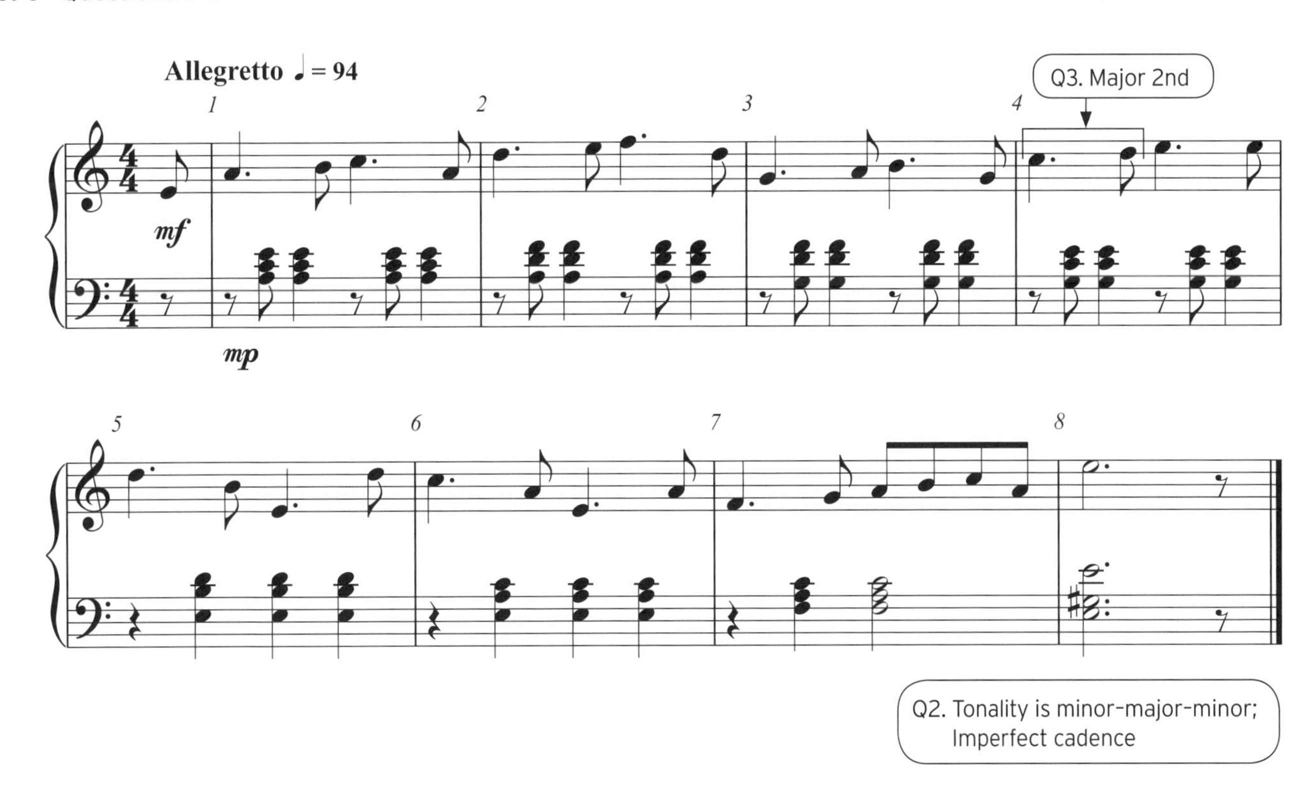

Question 4 (changed version)

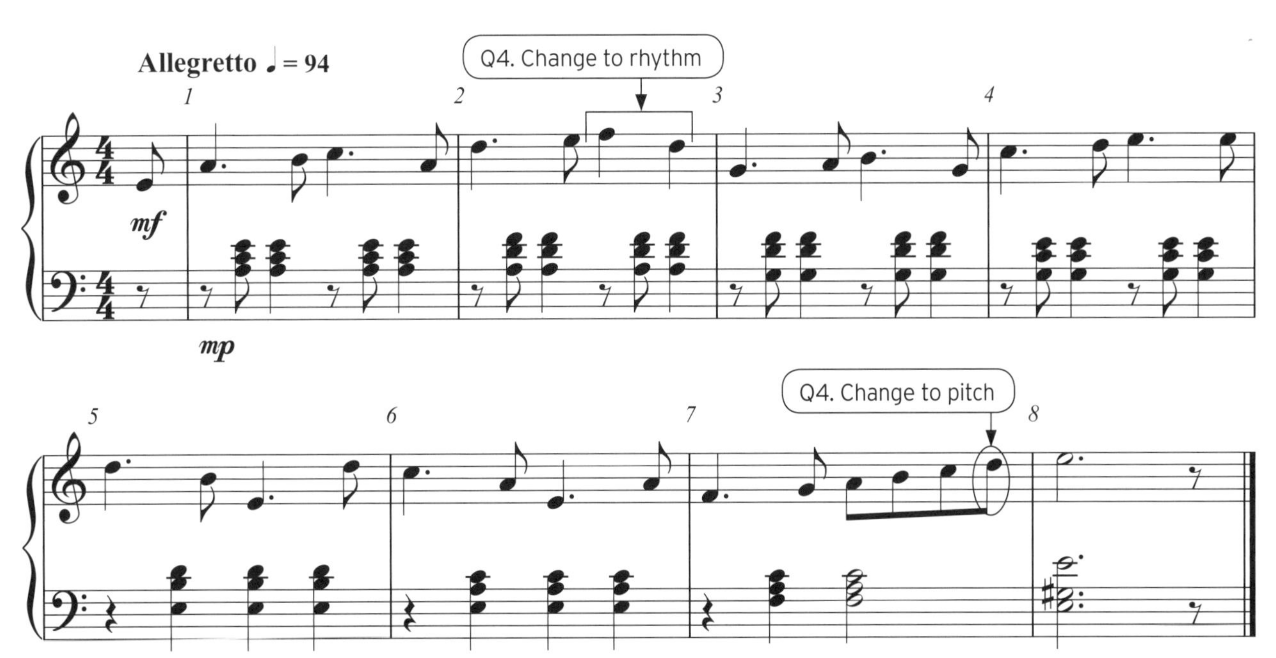

Test 7 Questions 1–4

Question 4 (changed version)

27

Test 8 Questions 1–4

Question 4 (changed version)

28

Test 9 Questions 1–4

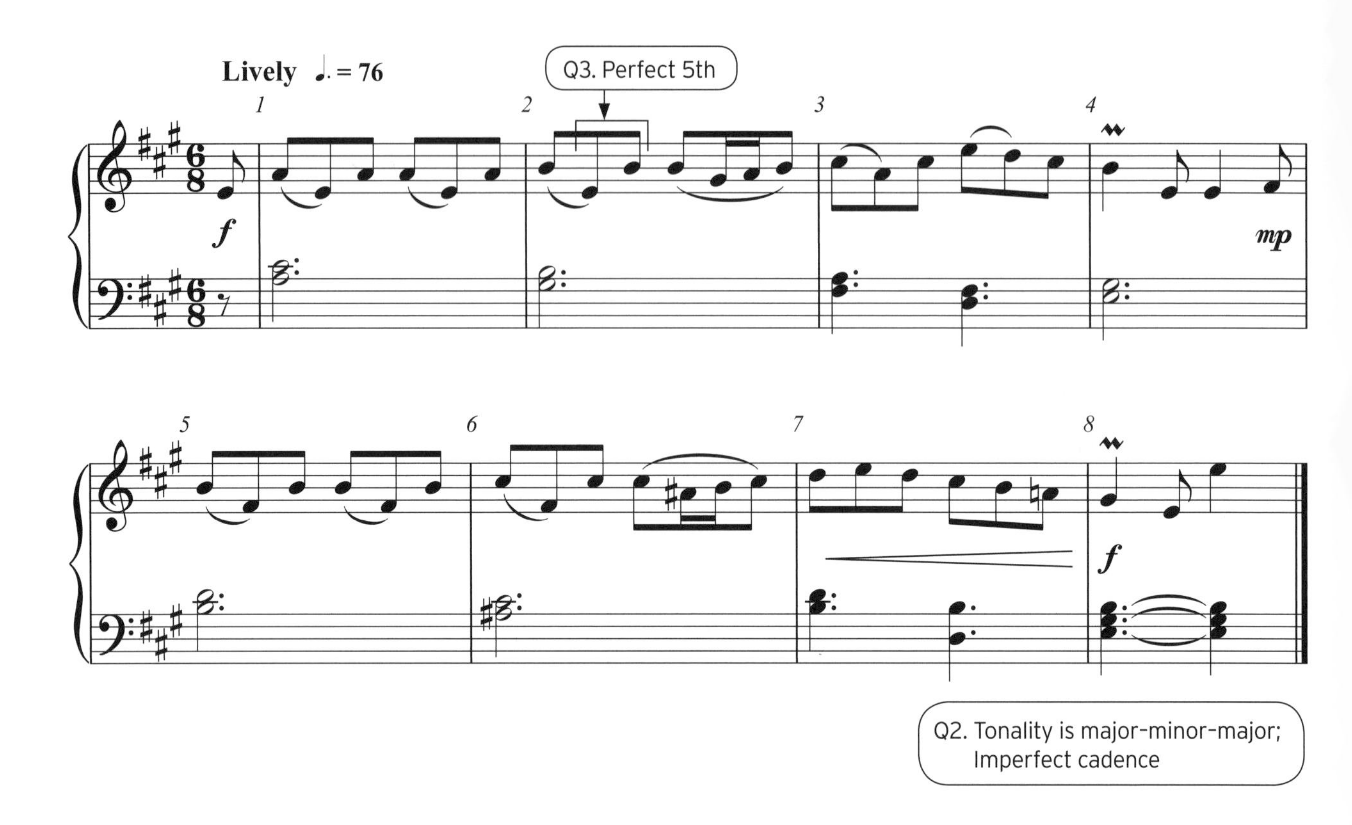

Question 4 (changed version)

Grade 4

About the test piece:

metre	$\frac{4}{4}$ or $\frac{6}{8}$
length	four bars
key	major or minor
style	piano style using treble and bass clefs
features	begins with a rising interval of a minor or major 2nd, minor or major 3rd, perfect 4th, perfect 5th, minor or major 6th; ends with either a perfect or imperfect cadence

All questions will be based on the same piece of music.

Question 1

What the examiner will do:

Play the piece twice.

What you will be asked to do:

Clap the pulse on the second playing, stressing the strong beat.

What the question is for:

- To learn to **recognise and respond to a regular pulse.**
- To recognise **where each bar begins.**
- To distinguish between **simple time** (beat easily divisible by 2) and **compound time** (beat easily divisible by 3).

Hints

- $\frac{4}{4}$ is an example of **simple time**. Each of the four beats in the bar is easily divisible into two shorter notes (♩ = ♫). Rhythms which fill a $\frac{4}{4}$ bar include 𝅗𝅥 ♩ ♩., ♩ ♫ ♩ ♫, ♩. ♪ ♩ ♩ and ♪♩ ♪ ♩. ♪
- $\frac{6}{8}$ is an example of **compound time**. Each of the two main beats in the bar is easily divisible into three shorter notes (♩. = ♪♪♪). As well as having three even quavers in each beat, compound time often uses the following rhythms: ♪. ♬ ♪ ♪. ♬ ♪ and ♩ ♪ ♩ ♪
- Many English nursery rhymes are in $\frac{6}{8}$, such as Humpty Dumpty, Hickory Dickory Dock, and Pop Goes the Weasel.
- Listen for the main beats in the bar and then try to listen to whether they can be divided into two or three. This will tell you whether the piece is in $\frac{4}{4}$ or $\frac{6}{8}$.

Hints

- Remember to make the first beat of each bar really clear by **clapping or tapping** it much more loudly than the other beat or beats. Remember, the examiner is looking to see if you **know where the strong beats are** as well as the speed of the pulse.
- At this grade you need to hear how the beats divide to be sure that you have the correct time signature.
- Remember that **the examiner will not ask you to name the time signature**, but will hear your answer from the pattern of your clapping.
- You don't have to wait until the second playing to try out your clapping. **You will be marked on the second playing only**, so you can try out your answer during the first playing.

Question 2

What the examiner will do:

Play the piece twice.

What you will be asked to do:

i) Tell the examiner whether the piece is in a **major or minor key.**

ii) Tell the examiner whether the piece ends with a **perfect cadence or an imperfect cadence.**

What the question is for:

- To develop your skills in **recognising major and minor keys** (tonality).
- To develop your skills in **recognising chord progressions** at the end of a piece.
- To learn the **words** to describe what you hear.

Hints

Tonality

- You need to be able to hear the difference between major and minor. See the **hints** at Grade 3 for further help if needed.

Cadences

- The **perfect cadence** is the only cadence at this grade that feels like a strong ending (full stop). It consists of a dominant chord (V) followed by a tonic chord (I or i).
- The **imperfect cadence** feels open-ended and unfinished, like a comma, or as if asking a question that needs an answering phrase. It consists of one of several chords followed by a dominant chord (V).
- The chord names are given for information: you only need to learn the names of the cadences, so concentrate on how they sound.

Question 3

What the examiner will do:

Play the first two notes of the melody once.

What you will be asked to do:

Name the interval made by the first two notes of the melody. The interval will be one of the following:

minor 2nd	minor 3rd	perfect 4th	perfect 5th	minor 6th
major 2nd	major 3rd			major 6th

What the question is for:

- To develop your skills in **recognising intervals** (the distance between notes).
- To learn the **words** to describe what you hear.

Hints

- At Grade 3 you identified intervals by number only (2nd, 3rd, 4th, 5th and 6th). **At this grade you need to give the interval names in full.** There are two parts to your answer: the numerical distance (2nd, 3rd, 4th, 5th or 6th) and the type of interval (major, minor or perfect).
- See Grade 3 for examples of major 2nd, major 3rd, perfect 4th, perfect 5th and major 6th intervals.
- The new intervals you will need to be able to recognise for Grade 4 are minor 2nd, minor 3rd and minor 6th.
- A minor 2nd sounds the same as a semitone. In a major scale there are minor 2nds between the 3rd & 4th degrees and between the 7th & 8th degrees:

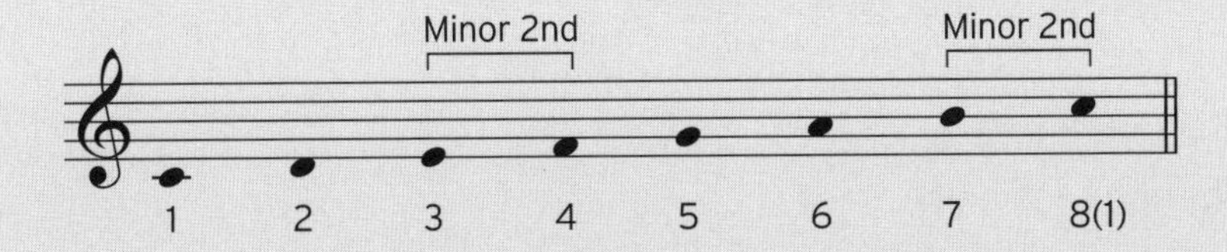

- The first two notes of a major arpeggio demonstrate a major 3rd. Similarly, the first two notes of a minor arpeggio demonstrate a minor 3rd:

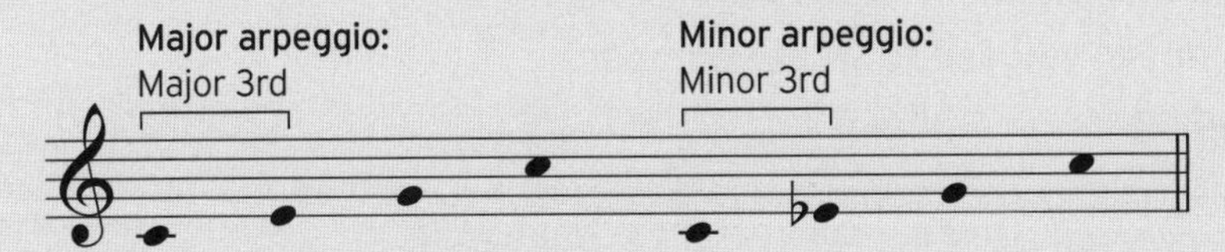

- You can also find intervals of a minor 3rd and a minor 6th in major arpeggios:

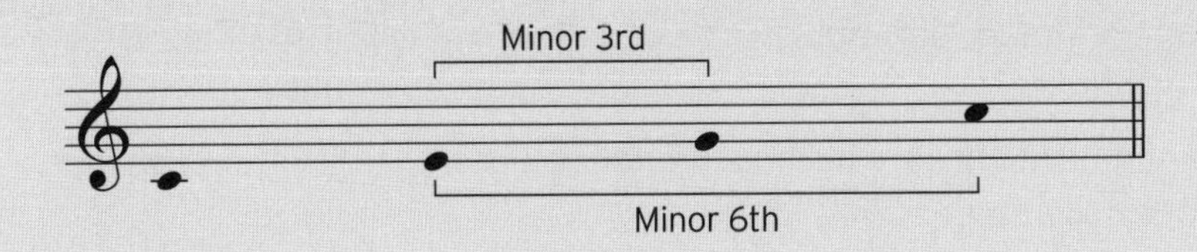

Hints

- Here are some tunes that start with these intervals. Try to find some others.

Minor 2nd

A Hard Day's Night
Jaws theme
Ode to Joy (second and third notes)
The Pink Panther theme
White Christmas

Minor 3rd

Greensleeves
Hello Dolly
Mack the Knife
Somewhere Out There (from *An American Tail*)
So Long, Farewell (from *The Sound of Music*)

Minor 6th

Chopin Waltz in C# minor, op. 64 no. 2
Close Every Door (from *Joseph and the Amazing Technicolor Dreamcoat*)
Let My People Go
Love Story theme (third and fourth notes)
The Entertainer (third and fourth notes)

- If it helps, **don't forget to sing or hum the notes** out loud before you answer in the exam.
- The intervals for this test will always be played from low note to high note (ie ascending).

Question 4

What the examiner will do:

- Give you a printed copy of the melody only.
- Play the melody twice, first as printed and then in a version with two changes, one to the rhythm and one to the pitch.

What you will be asked to do:

i) Identify the bar in which the **rhythm change** took place.
ii) Identify the bar in which the **pitch change** took place.

What the question is for:

- To develop your **musical memory**.
- To develop your **awareness of rhythm and pitch**.
- To develop your skills in **relating the music you see to what you hear**.
- To improve the **accuracy of your reading**.

Hints

- You will already have heard the original version **five** times before hearing the changed version.
- Try to concentrate on **listening** to the melody while you are following the printed music.
- Concentrate on the shape of the melody and look out for the places where what you hear does not match what you are looking at.
- Either use the printed copy to point to the bar in which each change occurs, or tell the examiner the bar numbers where the changes occur.
- Remember that **you are not allowed to make any marks on the copy of the music** you have been given, **or make any other notes during the test**. You could point your finger at the first change to help you remember where it was while you look and listen for the second change.
- If you play an instrument that usually uses bass or alto clef you can **ask for a copy of the melody in the clef you normally use**.

Try the tests

CD2 11 - 19

Listen to the CD or ask your teacher to play the tests for you. Each track on the CD contains a complete set of questions. The answers to the tests can be found on pages 18–22 of the **Answer Booklet.**

Printed below is the music you need for Question 4 of each set. Don't look at the music until you reach Question 4.

If you want to practise Question 4 using bass or alto clef, copies of the melodies can be downloaded from www.trinitycollege.com/music

Music for Grade 4 Question 4

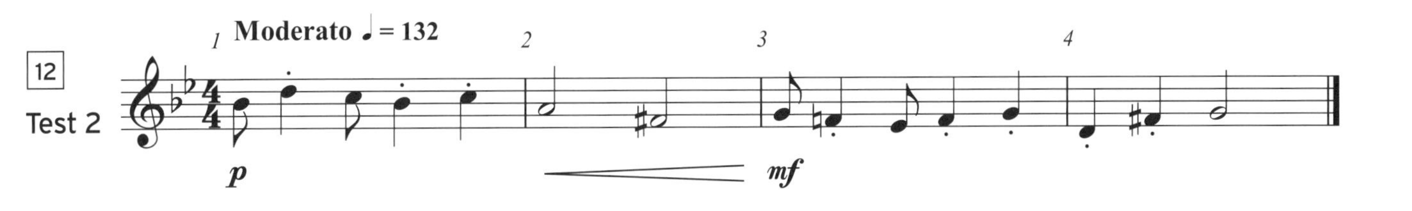

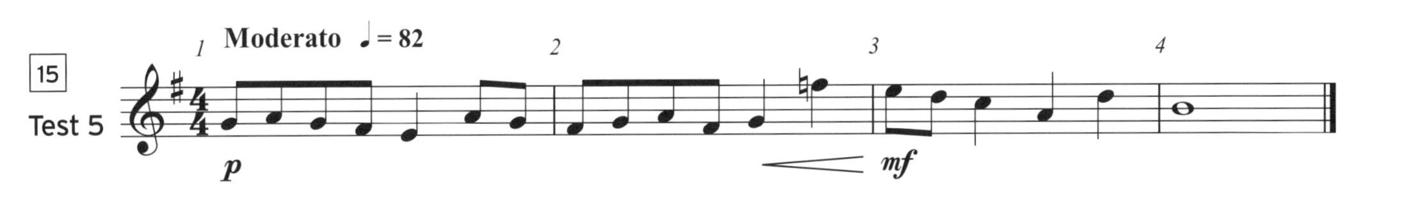

16
Test 6
Allegro ♩ = 108
1
2
3
4
f
mp
f

17
Test 7
Moderato ♩. = 60
1
2
3
4
mp
f

18
Test 8
Allegretto ♩ = 108
1
2
3
4
mf
mp

19
Test 9
Allegretto ♩. = 60
1
2
3
4
f

Grade 5

About the test piece:

metre	$\frac{2}{4}$, $\frac{3}{4}$, $\frac{4}{4}$ or $\frac{6}{8}$
length	eight bars
key	major or minor
style	piano style using treble and bass clefs
features	contains major-minor-major or minor-major-minor tonality; ends with a perfect, plagal, imperfect or interrupted cadence

All questions will be based on the same piece of music.

Question 1

What the examiner will do:

Play the piece twice.

What you will be asked to do:

i) Clap the pulse on the second playing, stressing the strong beat.

ii) Identify the time signature.

What the question is for:

- To learn to recognise and respond to a regular pulse.
- To distinguish between simple time ($\frac{2}{4}$, $\frac{3}{4}$ or $\frac{4}{4}$) and compound time ($\frac{6}{8}$).
- To recognise **where each bar begins.**
- To learn to recognise the time signature of a piece.

Hints

- All the time signatures that you need to know for this question have been covered in previous grades, but now you need to identify the time signature as well as clapping the pulse. See the **hints** for Grades 1–4 if you need to revise these.
- Make sure that you **make the first beat of each bar really clear** by clapping or tapping it much more loudly than the other beat or beats. Remember, the examiner is listening to hear if you know where the strong beats are as well as the speed of the pulse.
- **You don't have to wait until the second playing to try out your clapping.** The first playing is your chance to work out the time signature. You will be marked on the second playing only, so you can try out your answer during the first playing.

Question 2

What the examiner will do:

Play the piece twice.

What you will be asked to do:

i) Identify the tonality at the start of the piece, and explain the changes of tonality during the piece.
ii) Tell the examiner whether the cadence at the end of the piece is perfect, plagal, imperfect or interrupted.

What the question is for:

- To develop your skills in **recognising major and minor keys.**
- To develop your skills in **recognising key changes (modulations).**
- To develop your skills in **recognising chord progressions** at the end of pieces.
- To learn the **words** to describe what you hear.

Hints

Tonality

- You need to be able to hear the difference between major and minor. See the **hints** at Grades 3 and 4 for further help if needed.
- You also need to be able to listen for changes of key. As soon as a foreign note (chromatic note) is played, there is a sudden added colour to the music. This usually means that the music is travelling to a new key.
- The music will either start in a major key, travel to a minor key and return to the major key, or it will start in a minor key, travel to a major key and return to the minor key.
- The music will inevitably pass through a range of major and minor chords (like a train passing through stations). These are not necessarily modulations. You are listening for when the music definitely arrives at a new key (like a train stopping at a station).

Cadences

- At Grade 4 you learnt how to recognise **perfect** cadences (finished) and **imperfect** cadences (unfinished). At this grade you will need to be able to distinguish between **perfect, plagal, imperfect and interrupted** cadences.
- The **perfect cadence** feels like a strong ending (full stop). It consists of a dominant chord (V) followed by a tonic chord (I or i).
- The **plagal cadence** also feels like an ending, but is slightly less assertive. It consists of a subdominant chord (IV or iv) followed by a tonic chord (I or i).
- The **imperfect cadence** feels open-ended and unfinished, like a comma, or as if asking a question that needs an answering phrase. It consists of one of several chords followed by a dominant chord (V). Note that the final chord (V) is always major.
- The **interrupted cadence** feels like it is going to finish but has a surprise final chord. It consists of a dominant chord (V) followed by a submediant chord (vi or VI). An interrupted cadence in a major key will finish on a minor chord, and in a minor key will finish on a major chord.
- The chord names are given for information; you only need to learn the names of the cadences, so concentrate on how they sound.

Question 3

What the examiner will do:

Play two notes from the melody consecutively.

What you will be asked to do:

Name the interval, which will be one of the following:

minor 2nd	minor 3rd	perfect 4th	perfect 5th	minor 6th	minor 7th	octave
major 2nd	major 3rd			major 6th	major 7th	

What the question is for:

- To develop your skills in **recognising intervals** (the distances between notes).
- To learn the **words** to describe what you hear.

Hints

- Look at the hints for Grade 4, question 3. The same hints apply for this question, except that you also need to be able to recognise the minor 7th, major 7th and octave.
- At this grade you will need to learn to recognise every interval between two notes within an octave, except for the augmented 4th or diminished 5th (tritone).
- Singing intervals is the best way to learn to recognise them. To help you recognise a minor 7th, sing up a dominant 7th arpeggio. The first and fourth notes are a minor 7th apart:

- Practise singing a major 7th by singing up an octave first and then singing down a semitone:

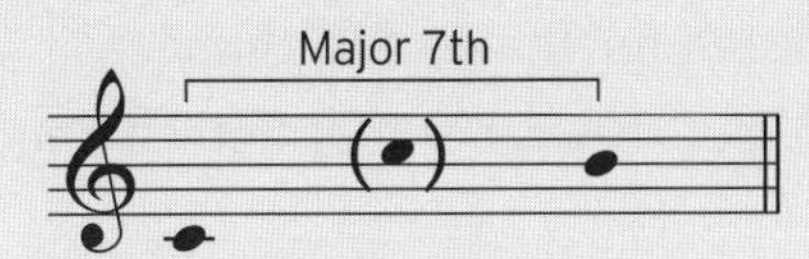

- Here are some tunes which start with these intervals. Try to find some others.

Minor 7th

Star Trek theme
Somewhere (from *West Side Story*)
The Winner Takes It All (second and third notes)

Major 7th

Bali Ha'i (from *South Pacific*) (first and third notes)
Don't Know Why (Norah Jones)
Somewhere over the Rainbow (first and third notes)
Take On Me (A-Ha)

Octave

Somewhere over the Rainbow
Singin' in the Rain
The Christmas Song
I Was Born to Love You (Queen)

- If it helps, don't forget to sing or hum the notes out loud before you answer in the exam.
- The intervals will always be played from low note to high note (ie ascending).

Question 4

What the examiner will do:

- Give you a printed copy of the piece.
- Play the piece twice, first as printed and then in a version with two changes, one to the rhythm and one to the pitch. Both changes will appear in the top line.

What you will be asked to do:

i) Identify the bar in which the **rhythm change** took place.
ii) Identify the bar in which the **pitch change** took place.

What the question is for:

- To develop your **musical memory.**
- To develop your **awareness of rhythm and pitch.**
- To develop your skills in **relating the music you see to what you hear.**
- To improve the **accuracy of your reading.**

Hints

- You will already have heard the original version **five** times before hearing the changed version.
- Try to concentrate on listening to the melody while you are following the printed music.
- Concentrate on the shape of the melody and look out for the places where what you hear does not match what you are looking at.
- Either use the printed copy to point to the bar in which each change occurs, or tell the examiner the bar numbers where the changes occur.
- Remember that **you are not allowed to make any marks on the copy of the music** you have been given, **or make any other notes during the test**. You could point your finger at the first change to help you remember where it was while you look and listen for the second change.
- At this grade you will hear the whole piece (not just the melody), but remember that both changes will be in the melody line.

Try the tests

CD2 20 - 28

Listen to the CD or ask your teacher to play the tests on the piano for you. Each track on the CD contains a complete set of questions.

Printed opposite is the music you need for Question 4 of each set. Don't look at the music until you reach Question 4.

The answers to the tests can be found on pages 24-32 of the **Answer Booklet.**

Music for Grade 5 Question 4

Test 3

23

Test 4

24
Test 5
Con moto ♩ = 104
mp
cresc.
f
25
Test 6
Allegretto ♩. = 94
mf
mp

26

Test 7

27

Test 8

Test 9

Information for teachers

Instrumentation

In the exam the tests will be played on the piano. In lessons they may be played live or delivered using the CD. Teachers should note that, although intended primarily for the piano, all tests from Initial to Grade 3 (and some at Grades 4 and 5) can also be played on any single-line melody instrument.

The questions

The four questions asked at each grade cover the following areas:

Metre and pulse

Candidates need to develop their recognition of evenly grouped beats, emphasis, rhythmic patterns and relative note lengths. At Initial they need to recognise $\frac{2}{4}$ time, at Grades 1-2 they distinguish between $\frac{2}{4}$ and $\frac{3}{4}$, at Grade 3 they distinguish between $\frac{3}{4}$ and $\frac{4}{4}$, at Grade 4 between $\frac{4}{4}$ and $\frac{6}{8}$, and at Grade 5 between all of the time signatures previously met. In this way all common time signatures are covered cumulatively.

At all levels covered in this book, candidates are required to clap the pulse of the test piece, stressing the strong beat. Candidates should be sure to emphasise the first beat of each bar very clearly, as the examiner will be using candidates' responses to assess their ability to detect the time signature of the music.

Teachers needing extension material for this question can of course use suitable melodies from other grades.

Perception of pitch

Beginning with questions about relative pitch over an increasing number of bars, by Grade 3 candidates need to recognise major and perfect intervals up to a 6th. The range of intervals is extended to include minor 2nds, 3rds and 6ths at Grade 4, and at Grade 5 any interval within an octave may be included, with the exception of the tritone. As long as the parameters of the grade are observed, any parts of any melodies may provide suitable extension material, and students can be encouraged to be aware of the intervals encountered in the pieces they are playing or singing. The examples of well-known instances of particular intervals given in this book can be adapted to suit each student's individual cultural background and/or musical interests.

From Grade 3 tonality is explored, at first by asking if the test piece was major or minor, and introducing changing tonality at Grade 5.

Recognition of perfect and imperfect cadences is introduced at Grade 4, and at Grade 5 candidates are expected to recognise all four cadences.

Characteristics of performance

At Initial and Grades 1 and 2, questions are asked about dynamics, with variation in dynamics introduced at Grade 2. Questions are asked about articulation at Initial and Grades 1 and 2. Candidates' awareness of dynamics and articulation should grow from their own playing, and the appropriate vocabulary and discussion of performance practice and interpretation encouraged from the start. These exercises can easily be extended by reversing the element(s) asked about, or by otherwise varying the material. Students who are unfamiliar with the sound of the piano will need to experience how differing dynamics and articulations will sound, and should note that contrast in these elements is built into each test.

Perception of change

From Grade 1 candidates will be asked questions relating to changes made by the examiner to the test piece, which by this stage in the test will have been heard a number of times. In addition, from Grade 3 upwards candidates are shown a copy of the test piece and asked to locate and explain changes made to it in subsequent playings. This question draws together elements covered in previous questions; developing musical memory (of pitch and rhythm) over an increasing timescale, recognising characteristics in a piece of music and making judgements about it, as well as improving candidates' reading skills and developing their ear-to-eye links.

The demands of this question increase in a carefully structured way, beginning with simply locating a change at Grade 1, to discriminating between changes of pitch and rhythm at Grade 2, then moving on at Grade 3 to include the use of the score to locate a change. From Grade 4 two changes must be located and explained, and at Grade 5 the single-line melody is replaced by the complete piece (although changes remain in the melody line only).

Marking

In all exams the aural tests are worth 10% of the total marks available. Marks for the aural tests are awarded holistically; that is without a fixed number of marks being allotted to each question. This enables examiners to indicate not only whether answers were correct, but also to give due credit to promptness and confidence of response. In general, all questions should be regarded as equally important in terms of marking.

Full assessment criteria are available from Trinity's website www.trinitycollege.com

Track listing

CD 1

Grade	Test	Track no.
Initial	1	01
	2	02
	3	03
	4	04
	5	05
	6	06
	7	07
	8	08
	9	09
	10	10
	11	11
	12	12
	13	13
	14	14
Grade 1	1	15
	2	16
	3	17
	4	18
	5	19
	6	20
	7	21
	8	22
	9	23
	10	24
	11	25
	12	26
	13	27
	14	28
Grade 2	1	29
	2	30
	3	31
	4	32
	5	33
	6	34
	7	35
	8	36
	9	37
	10	38
	11	39
	12	40
	13	41

CD 2

Grade	Test	Track no.
Grade 3	1	01
	2	02
	3	03
	4	04
	5	05
	6	06
	7	07
	8	08
	9	09
	10	10
Grade 4	1	11
	2	12
	3	13
	4	14
	5	15
	6	16
	7	17
	8	18
	9	19
Grade 5	1	20
	2	21
	3	22
	4	23
	5	24
	6	25
	7	26
	8	27
	9	28

Produced and engineered by Ken Blair
Recorded at Red Gables Studio

Piano: Peter Wild
Voiceover: Luise Horrocks